I don't want to be inside me anymore

I don't want to be inside me anymore

MESSAGES FROM AN AUTISTIC MIND

BIRGER SELLIN

TRANSLATED BY ANTHEA BELL

With an Introduction by Michael Klonovsky

BasicBooks
A Division of HarperCollins*Publishers*

Designed by Barbara DuPree Knowles

LIBRARY OF CONGRESS CATALOGING-IN-PUBLICATION DATA

Sellin, Birger.

[Ich will kein in mich mehr sein.   English]

I don't want to be inside me anymore : messages from an autistic

mind / Birger Sellin ; translated by Anthea Bell ; with an

introduction by Michael Klonovsky.

p.   cm.

Includes bibliographical references.

ISBN 0–465–03172–2

1. Sellin, Birger—Psychology.   2. Autistic children—Germany—

Case studies.   3. Autistic children—Language—Case studies.

4. Facilitated communication—Case studies.   I. Title.

RJ506.A9S45513   1995

618.92´898209—dc20

94–38354

CIP

95 96 97 98 ◆/HC 9 8 7 6 5 4 3 2 1

now i am going to write a song about the joy of
    speaking
a song for mute autistics to sing in institutions and
    madhouses
nails in forked branches are the instruments
i am singing the song from deep down in hell i am
    calling
out to all the silent people in this world
make this song your song
thaw out the icy walls
make sure you arent thrown out
we will be a new generation of mute people
a whole crowd of us singing new songs
songs such as speaking people have never heard
of all the poets i dont know of one who was mute
so we will be the first
and people wont be able to shut their ears to our
    singing
im writing for my silent sisters
for my silent brothers
we want people to hear us and give us somewhere
we can live among all of you
live a life in this society

Birger Sellin
September 21, 1992

I don't want to be inside me anymore

Introduction

by Michael Klonovsky

One day in early February 1992, I got a telephone call from a friend, a lawyer who works in the Superior Court of Justice in Berlin. "You're a journalist," he said. "I know you're always looking for interesting stories—I think I have one for you. A colleague of mine has a nineteen-year-old son who's autistic; he hasn't spoken a word since he was two. He had been considered mentally retarded, a hopeless case—until he suddenly began writing. Now this young man—his name is Birger Sellin—sits at his computer every evening writing this amazing stuff."

"What do you mean, *autistic?*"

"Haven't you seen that movie *Rain Man?*"

"No."

"Okay, then, . . . autism," my friend began, pausing to gather his thoughts, "autism is an extraordinary disability. Autistic people can't make contact with their environment. They withdraw into themselves and don't seem to register anything that goes on around them."

"And someone like that suddenly starts writing?"

"Yes, that's just it! You absolutely must read his stuff. The boy's amazing!"

My curiosity was aroused. I knew nothing at all about autism, but I decided to look into it. My decision may

1

have been made partly out of instinctive sympathy for a person who removed himself entirely from the world—a notion that didn't seem so strange to me. (Later, I came to realize that such glib ideas about autism don't hold up at all and, moreover, are regarded with great cynicism by autistics themselves.) I dug into the press archives for recent pieces on autism, and I consulted two Berlin psychologists who treated people suffering from this affliction. Gradually, I came to realize that it lay far beyond anything I had ever experienced.

I discovered that autistic people live like prisoners in the dungeons of their own minds. For unexplained reasons, they shut themselves off from the world in early childhood, usually before the age of three. Despite a wealth of biological, genetic, and psychological theories about the origins of autism—from prenatal brain injury to faulty mothering—no one really knows what causes it or how best to treat it. In fact, in the words of Birger's therapist, Margard Breinlinger, "the more you put your mind to autism, the less clear the picture becomes."

Typically, autistic children cannot relate emotionally to anyone, even their parents. They avoid all body and eye contact and act as if they were deaf, either not speaking at all or merely echoing what is said to them. They do not play like other children; they repeat the same movements mechanically and fall into fits of raging frenzy if anything unexpected occurs in their environment. During these fits they may inflict painful injuries on themselves. However, I learned, these are only external symptoms. No one really knows what goes on in an autistic person's head.

I learned too that many autistics are not mentally retarded, and may even be highly intelligent, but their inability to communicate makes it extremely difficult to assess their mental capacities. The prospects of a cure are poor, and as a result adult autistics whose parents can no longer shoulder the burden of caring for them often live out their lives in custodial care. Autism is a riddle that has yet to be solved. It is so poorly understood that it is often misdiagnosed as schizophrenia, mental retardation, even deafness. We do know that it affects about four times as many boys as girls, and that it is rare in primitive societies. The Dutch behavioral scientists Elisabeth and Niko Tinbergen call autism one of the most complicated natural phenomena in existence.

I became more and more eager to meet a member of this strange group. Feeling at least partly prepared after my preliminary research, I got in touch with Birger's parents. Annemarie and Dankward Sellin were very interested in publicizing their son's story and wanted me to meet him. I told them that first I'd like to read what Birger had written, and they mailed it to me.

I was stunned. These were not the ramblings of a person isolated from his fellow humans, but a cry for help from an incomprehensible, dismal world. The writings seemed to emerge from a state of great distress. Deeply sad, full of loneliness and mystery, they had been written in extraordinarily powerful language. They reminded me of Nietzsche, Hölderlin, Artaud, or the old Norse verse epics.

Fascinated, I read through the two hundred pages again and again. A few days later I made an appointment to visit the Sellins in their small house on the southern outskirts of Berlin. I wanted to learn something about Birger's environment before I met him.

I arrived about noon. Birger was still at the center for

young autistics run by the German Society for Autistic Children, where he spends the main part of the day. He would not be home before four o'clock, his mother told me. I didn't mind, since this would give me time to explore the terrain at my leisure. I was apprehensive about meeting Birger; I didn't know how to act toward him. Birger's mother assured me it would be best to act perfectly normal and natural. I talked to Annemarie and Dankward for a while and looked around the house. There was nothing to indicate that anyone unusual lived there.

Birger's parents left me in the living room to reread some of his pieces. Alone in the room, I pondered his words: "i would so much like to find the way out of my isolated life out of the weird behavior i use like armor i feel so frustrated day in day out without hope its like being buried alive the loneliness of an autistic is like a great clod of earth weighing down the soul. . . ."

Suddenly the door opened with a violent jerk and Birger stormed into the room. When he saw me, he flinched and stopped in his tracks. Tall and burly, but at the same time seeming to shrink into himself in a strange way, Birger stood a few paces from me, his stained sweater hanging out of his trousers. His restless, wavering glance left me and wandered around the room. Then, snorting, he walked around the table where I was sitting and flung himself on the sofa. Taking no further notice of me, he started rocking the upper part of his body monotonously while staring into space. Lower jaw jutting, he puffed air into his own face. His breathing became heavier and heavier, gradually turning into a loud panting. After a while he slipped to the floor, where several hundred marbles and glass beads were scattered about. Birger scooped up a handful of them and let them run through his oddly crooked fingers into a plastic beaker, a process he kept repeating. Now and then his panting was interrupted by a deep groan, somewhere between pleasure and pain, while the marbles kept rattling to the floor.

For a moment I was paralyzed. Could this pitiable, apparently feebleminded young man really be the author of the writings lying in front of me? Can a human being's outward appearance and intellect be in such striking contrast? How could this strange boy dropping marbles on the floor as if his life depended on it have not only a spark of intelligence but remarkable literary gifts?

I watched Birger for a while, reviewing in my mind what I knew about him: he does not have himself under control; he can't speak but he can read and write; he understands everything I say and registers everything I do; he lives, as it were, somewhere inside this person whose behavior seems so odd to me.

I swallowed my astonishment and spoke to him; I told him I was fascinated by what he had written and that I would like to write about him. No reaction. Compulsively, I went on talking, determined not to let this meeting throw me off balance. As I droned on, Birger became increasingly restless. Suddenly he struck his face several times with the heel of his right hand and began to scream. I watched helplessly as he screamed louder and louder, biting his hands the whole time. Then he suddenly left the room, slamming the door behind him. His high, shrill screams rang through the entire house.

That was February 26, 1992. Since then I have come to understand more about the world of Birger Sellin and other autistic people. More than anything else, Birger's own writings have given me insight.

After that first meeting, I visited Birger several times at his home, I went to the center where he spends his days, and I talked to his parents and other people who know him, trying to construct a picture of his life. The mysterious and ominous first impression Birger made on me soon gave way to a more complex view. In time, I came to see that Birger's face has regular features; they become twisted and distorted only under the influence of the storm raging deep inside him. I no longer think it odd to see someone of his intelligence playing with marbles. However, the great gulf between Birger's writings and his outward appearance is still as incomprehensible to me as ever.

On July 31, 1992, five months after I first met Birger, the Hamburg magazine *Die Zeit* published an article about him. It was at that point that his parents first expressed a wish to tell the world about Birger's writings, which were increasing in number every day. This book embodies that wish. Not only has Birger expressed a strong desire to see it published, but he has followed its progress closely. Of course, even more important to Birger than the publication of this book is his wish to overcome his autism and find a place for himself in society. Like his parents and all of us who know Birger, I very much hope he will succeed. The publicity from that first magazine article, and from others published since then, seems to have been of considerable help; Birger has received dozens of letters and presents, as well as several offers from publishing and film companies.

Over the last few years several books have appeared written by autistics who describe how they have managed to overcome their affliction. Although these people are not cured, they have learned to cope with their handicap and lead relatively independent lives. Birger Sellin's story is very different from theirs. He is still enslaved by his disability, sending messages to us from his autistic prison. Despite his enormous capacity to absorb information and his descriptive talent, Birger is considered one of the most severe cases of autism in Germany today. His world is unimaginably remote from ours. It is something of a miracle that messages from that world reach us at all. At the same time, Birger's language has its own aesthetic value, and the authenticity of that language, born of great pain, is something that a writer without his handicap might never be able to achieve.

FALLING SILENT

Disaster struck young Birger before he was two years old. In the last few months of his second year, he disappeared into another world, one from which he has not yet found his way back. I can describe the outward circumstances in which Birger sank into autism, but no one knows just how or why it happened.

Birger was born on February 1, 1973, in West Berlin, the first child of Annemarie Sellin, a teacher of religious instruction, and Dankward Sellin, a law student. His early development and behavior were perfectly normal, with no sign of any psychological trouble. On the contrary: Birger was an outgoing, happy, and greatly loved child who began to talk at a very early age.

In October 1974 Birger's parents sent him to nursery school on a trial basis. He was to attend for two hours in the mornings, so he could get used to it. But when his parents came to pick him up at midday he screamed "bloody murder," as his mother put it, and couldn't be calmed down. When the same thing happened the next day, the Sellins decided to keep their son at home.

Soon after that Birger became sick. For several weeks he suffered from a recurrent middle ear inflammation and from bouts of vomiting. Three months later he seemed to have recovered, but by then he was a different child. He screamed after every afternoon nap and whenever he had to leave the house, and he panicked at the sight of other children. At the same time his command of language began to deteriorate until all he could do was stammer single words. His vocabulary shrank steadily, and one day he stopped talking entirely. He no longer responded to his parents, and he avoided all eye contact. The Sellins looked on helplessly as their child withdrew from them, turning completely in on himself.

The first doctor Annemarie and Dankward consulted saw no reason for concern: it was only an interruption of development, he said. But when the "interruption" persisted, the boy's parents took him to other doctors. Birger's head was painstakingly investigated. He was X-rayed and CAT-scanned, all to no avail.

In October 1975, just one year after his disastrous experience at the nursery school, Birger's parents took him to the Wiesengrund Psychiatric Hospital for Children and Young People in Berlin. They had to leave him there, they were told, for six weeks of inpatient therapy. Reluctantly they agreed, a move Dankward Sellin would later term "a great mistake."

The six weeks became six months. Birger's parents were persuaded to allow this extended treatment by the invariable excuse they were given that Birger hadn't "yet made much progress," by the prospect of a cure that was dangled before them, and by the direct, cynical question, "What else are you going to do with the boy?" Birger seemed apathetic during their daily visits, although his mother recalls that "he did seem glad to see us."

Birger made no apparent progress under treatment. After six months of therapy a case report diagnosed him as "probably suffering from postencephalitic retardation," that is, mental retardation brought on by an inflammation of the brain cells. The Sellins felt more helpless than ever. When Birger returned from the hospital, they took turns staying home with him. Not able to communicate with them or react to anything, he sat impassively in the living room, constantly rocking his upper body.

Finally, Birger's parents were able to get him accepted into a kindergarten for children with motor disturbances, although his disability was much more complicated than that. Once his parents saw some of the other children there jabbing Birger with sticks to try to make him talk. "He must have grown his armor bit by bit," recalls Annemarie Sellin. However, Birger's time at the Friedenau kindergarten did produce one ray of hope. Given flash cards to arrange, he performed at lightning speed, suggesting that he still had cognitive faculties.

At home, he spent most of his time absorbed in the rigid, repetitive action of leafing through books he would pull down from his parents' shelves. Birger was always surrounded by books; he would thumb through them jerkily, cracking their spines and sometimes destroying them. Sometimes his parents felt as if he were walling himself up behind piles of books. Even when the books were replaced by building blocks, Birger continued to build walls around himself.

When Birger was four and a half his parents, on the advice of a psychologist friend, took him to the hospital of the Free University of Berlin to be examined. It was here that they first heard about autism, a disability almost unknown in Germany at the time. Birger's diagnosis was "infantile autism," then considered an incurable condition.

This diagnosis radically altered the lives of Annemarie and Dankward Sellin. From then on it looked as if careers, vacations, evenings out with friends would be luxuries that at least one of them would have to forsake. Birger was not going to turn into a normal child who could be left alone or sent outside to play by himself.

In that year, 1977, the German Society for Autistic Children was established in West Berlin. At last, in the person of staff psychologist Margard Breinlinger, someone came into Birger's life "who understood him," says his mother. The boy attended the Society's Early Development program, where he learned to eat, wash, dress, brush his teeth, and go to the toilet by himself. His general health improved. His parents felt for the first time that their child was in good hands. Birger did not scream when his parents left him at the institution, and he seemed to feel at home there.

Over the next few years Birger went through all six stages of the Society's program (arranged by age), attending the institution every day for six hours. Gradually, he became relatively independent. His parents could take him for walks or out shopping with them. Birger also began to do small chores around the house. But he still did not speak a word, and he remained at the developmental stage of a toddler.

During this time, Birger dropped his seemingly aimless manipulation of books in favor of a new type of mechanical repetition, which soon became his chief occupation: running marbles and glass beads through his hands for hours on end, as if hypnotized. Outdoors, he played the game with similar intensity, trickling sand instead of marbles through his fingers.

At home, Birger's favorite place was underneath the dining table in the living room. He obviously felt safest there. Apart from the absence of any sign of intellectual development, he gave his parents few problems. He had adapted to his environment to the point of becoming inconspicuous. When his mother entertained her fellow students (from 1977 to 1982 she studied psychology at the Free University in Berlin), Birger would sit under the table for hours playing with marbles, drawing no attention to himself. When he was six his parents were even able to take him to Crete on vacation.

The therapists at the center were baffled by Birger's dogged refusal to develop in any way. Small signs of progress—for instance, copying painted stripes or building a tower of wooden blocks—were celebrated as successes, but he kept taking them right back to the start of their therapy. From the age of eight the autistic children in the center were given specialized lessons. Birger's total lack of interest in these lessons was thought to show that he found them too demanding, so the level of the tasks was always being lowered for him.

Birger's parents, despite their son's apparent lack of comprehension, sometimes had the uncanny feeling that Birger was watching them and understood what was going on. The idea that intelligence might be latent in his strange, withdrawn nature was suggested by Birger's relationship with his marbles. Although he had hundreds of marbles and glass beads, he seemed to notice instantly if a single one was missing: he would become restless and search frantically for it. The marbles also provided the occasion for the only sentence Birger has so far uttered. When his father, playing with him, took one of the marbles, Birger demanded in a strong, clear voice, "Give me that ball back!" Dankward Sellin was thunderstruck. Annemarie cried out and came running in from the next room. For days the parents urged their son to speak again. But it was no use. He retreated into his silence and isolation.

THE INNER LIFE
OF THE AUTISTIC PERSON

The variety of theories about autism suggests that it may be a collective term for a syndrome that arises in different ways and manifests itself differently in each autistic person. What is true for one may not apply to another at all. There are autistics who lead restricted but fairly normal lives; there are apparently hopeless cases who cannot communicate at all; and there are those like Birger, who have communicative abilities in spite of severe disability, and who give us some small window into their lives.

Although it is difficult to understand the inner life of

any autistic person, we do know that imperfect adaptation and withdrawal are characteristic of the condition. Autistic children and adults experience everyday life as unpredictable and chaotic, and they are threatened by this chaos. Depending on the degree of their disability, they are unable to sort out their perceptions: it is as if they lack a filter for separating important from unimportant stimuli. The outside world assails autistic people with intense force. One autistic woman who later became "socialized" (rather than "cured") recalled that speech sounded to her "like a freight train racing at high speed."

Facing this barrage of impressions, an autistic child, for self-protection, develops mechanisms in early life for shutting out the outside world. The psychoanalyst Bruno Bettelheim noted that autistic children display utter defeatism in handling the outside world; instead of acting in a way that will get them results, all they can do is try to prevent any results from occurring.

Withdrawal goes hand in hand with loss of the ability to communicate. The basic way children get to know the world around them—through exploration and play—is all but closed off to autistic children. They explore their world extremely slowly, and only within strict limits. The socialization that unfolds unconsciously and automatically in a normal person is usually beyond the capacity of autistics because of their impaired ability to process information.

Much of what autistic children see and hear makes no sense to them. Unable to interpret what is going on around them or to recognize practical cause and effect, they live in a world that seems alien and threatening. They seem to cope with it by taking as little notice of it as possible and by remaining as inconspicuous in it as they can. Thus most autistics become distressed as soon as there are any changes around them that they cannot explain to themselves.

In reaction to the chaos they experience, autistic people create ritualized private worlds for themselves. These rituals vary in form, but they have one common purpose: to provide an internal security system, an island of order to withdraw to if need be (and the need is almost constant). Most notable are the various fixed, or "stereotyped," actions I have been describing. This *stereotypy*—along with indifference and introversion—is the most striking feature of autism. In fact, these mysterious modes of behavior are the only signals autistics send out. Their primitive nature has led observers to the mistaken assumption that all autistic people are mentally retarded. But the autistic person's apparently pointless behavior represents a unique adaptation, a deliberate avoidance mechanism that works as a defensive bulwark in front of the autistic fortress. Elisabeth and Niko Tinbergen have called stereotypy the central component of the autistic avoidance system.

To the observer, these repetitive actions do indeed look startling. One day, for example, when I visited Birger's day center, I was greeted by the following scene. A girl stood by the wall, swaying the upper part of her body from side to side with wide, sweeping movements. She kept her arms behind her back and rested her whole weight on one leg. Another girl, seated, spun a ball around in front of her like a top, standing up now and then to give the ball a series of hard bounces. A boy sat casually on the floor, legs outstretched, looking up at the ceiling and moving his raised head to one side at regular intervals. Birger sat among these three, playing with his marbles.

Other stereotypical actions include twirling, pacing up and down, leg swinging, rolling back and forth, waving objects in the air, and turning objects around and around. The Australian autistic Donna Williams describes this condition as "learning to lose myself in anything I desired." Stereotypy may also include childlike behavior: playing with food, playing water games in the bathroom, constantly switching the lights on and off. Autistic people who speak also frequently display linguistic stereotypy (echolalia), repeating the same words over and over or simply repeating what you say to them. The autistic girl at Birger's center who was playing with the ball came up to me and asked my name. When I introduced myself, she walked off, chanting my answer: "Michael. Michael. Michael." But even autistics who speak conceal their deeper levels of consciousness; the inner being is protected rather than revealed by language.

Silence—and at least one autistic person in three is mute—embodies even stronger self-protection. Even if nontalking autistics had the power of language—and that is indeed possible—what would they do with it? Elisabeth and Niko Tinbergen, who have spent years working with autistic children, conclude that an autistic child does not speak because, as a result of abnormal anxiety or the suppression of social contact, he or she either does not want to or does not dare to speak. As speech is a form of social contact, they say, it too must be inhibited if the entire system of social conduct is suppressed.

Stereotypical behaviors may serve more than a protective function. The neurologist Carl H. Delacato calls the ritual acts of an autistic person desperate cries for help. It has been observed that the intensity of stereotypical behavior increases when an autistic person feels threatened. The Tinbergens suspect that there is a permanent conflict of motivations behind these instances of stereotypy; the autistic wants to carry out some action but does not feel capable of doing so, and retreats. The stereotypical behavior channels the internal state of indecision to the outside world.

This way of reacting to conflict or anxiety is not unusual. We all react stereotypically to stress: we scratch our heads, bite our lips, move objects back and forth for no reason, tug nervously at our hair, tap our feet, draw deeply on cigarettes, pace up and down. But we can resolve this behavior with purposeful communication, whereas an autistic person may tear out her hair or bite his fingers until they bleed.

Another stereotypical pattern is maintaining a stable environment and a regular daily routine. If this rhythm is unexpectedly disturbed, autistics may become frantic and turn their aggression on themselves or (much more rarely) on others. The terrible injuries that autistics may inflict on themselves have contributed to the grotesque picture many people have of this disorder. But autistic people feel so threatened and helpless that it is as though they are teetering at the edge of a cliff, the slightest nudge being enough to send them tumbling. Understanding this may help us make sense of their behavior under stress.

Autistics may also react to nonthreatening situations with furious attacks on themselves. Often this is the only way they can express their displeasure when they feel misunderstood. Some will hurt themselves to get confirmation of their perception of themselves. Donna Williams writes that an autistic person may inflict self-harm "to test whether one is actually real. As no other person is experienced directly because all feeling gets held at some sort of mental checkpoint . . . it is easy to wonder whether one in fact exists."

In spite of their low degree of socialization and the retention of infantile behavior patterns, some autistic people have highly developed intellects. These are often isolated talents: the stunning mathematical ability or feats of memory that have given rise to the concept of the "idiot savant," a rather cruel French term now replaced by "autistic savant." These talents represent a mystery that developmental psychology has not yet succeeded in explaining.

Interestingly, the skills autistics pick up usually have no connection to their disturbed social behavior and are often things they teach themselves. The urge to create a system is obviously crucial. Like the physical stereotypical behavior to which even the most intelligent autistic person clings, the learning and constant recapitulation of self-contained thought patterns provide security.

The autistic condition can thus be described as a desperate search for order and regularity. Many autistics find mathematics or music more logical and easier to grasp than, for instance, going to the supermarket, which to them is a trip through chaos. We simply do not perceive the same complexity in the outside world; to us, the number of cars passing us on the way to the supermarket—a hundred, two hundred—is as unimportant as their color or how many different kinds of chocolate bars are on the shelf. But autistics have been known to panic if the breakfast table has too many objects, or unfamiliar objects, on it.

Many autistics have a vast ability to absorb information. In the 1960s a pair of autistic twins created a great sensation in the United States with their astounding memory for numbers. They flung prime numbers of ten to twenty figures back and forth between themselves as other children might volley a tennis ball, and, given random dates from the past or the future, they determined almost instantly what day of the week it would be. The twins were unable to do simple division, though, so it was assumed that they had eidetic, or photographic, memory and "saw" the numbers in their minds.

In the film *Rain Man,* which dramatically brought the phenomenon of the autistic savant to public attention, the title character, played by Dustin Hoffman, knew the telephone directory of an entire city by heart. This was not a Hollywood fantasy; many autistic people can memorize the contents of encyclopedias, textbooks, even phone directories. Professor Hans Kehrer of the Institute for Research into Autism in Münster describes an autistic man who could not tell time but knew more about brain physiology than his psychologist did. Others have an astonishing memory for pictures and can reproduce in drawings the most minute details of something they have seen. As we shall see, some of these remarkable traits apply to Birger Sellin as well.

The internal state of an autistic person can be thought of as a mixture of long-term stress, brought on by the constant feeling of anxiety, and deadly boredom. Bruno Bettelheim compares this anxiety to the intense fear felt just before death. Like the concentration camp inmates of the Nazi era, says Bettelheim, autistics are exposed to an extreme situation with the following typical factors: it cannot be avoided; its duration is uncertain; it represents a permanent threat to life, whether real or imagined; it makes future events seem unpredictable; and at the same time it leaves the person with an absolute inability to do anything about it.

We can only guess, with horror, how many autistic people have had to live out their lives undiagnosed in psychiatric hospitals (as some indeed still do), strapped down, pumped full of drugs, or locked up, before this syndrome and its characteristic features were even partially recognized and treated.

FACILITATED COMMUNICATION

On May 14, 1983, when Birger was ten years old, his brother, Jonas, was born. His parents were worried about Birger's reactions to this event, but Birger immediately made contact with Jonas and left no doubt that he fully accepted this new member of the family. "We never had a moment's concern about Jonas," says his mother. "We could leave him alone with Birger anytime."

Coping with Birger became more complicated with the coming of puberty, however. Up to then, he had behaved like a mute, relatively amenable child; now it became difficult to take him anywhere. Birger lived in an increasingly hectic state. He had screaming fits. He bit and hit himself until he drew blood. His breath rose in that violent manner I described earlier and often became a wild panting (probably a form of stereotypy to soothe himself). He ran frantically around the house, wet his bed, gorged himself on any food he could lay his hands on, and drove his parents to snap at him. All the while he remained mute, uninterested in anything, and apparently without real understanding of what was going on around him.

If Birger's screaming fits came on while he was out walking or in a store, he attracted crowds of people. Once when he and his mother were in Wittenbergplatz, in the middle of Berlin, he screamed for an hour nonstop. "It was pure hell," recalls Annemarie Sellin. His uncontrolled tantrums drove Birger's family into isolation. "We couldn't invite people over, keep up friendships, go away—we just had to live day by day," says Annemarie. Even Birger's stereotypical behavior no longer seemed to work as a tranquilizer. Looking back, Birger's father says: "He must have been in the depths of despair at this time."

At the age of sixteen Birger ran away from his parents for the first time, during a shopping trip to the Kaufhaus des Westens store. Workers at the store refused to use the loudspeaker system to help find him, saying it was not their policy. After several hours' search, the Sellins found their son; he had been taken to a hospital and was strapped to a stretcher. On another occasion Birger slipped out of his day center when no one was looking, boarded the first subway train that came along, and rode south. The police picked him up and took him to the hospital. When his parents, who had reported him missing, came to get him, they found him under police guard.

With growing despair, his parents watched their son becoming more and more uncontrollable. They hardly dared to think what the rest of his life would be like. By the time he was eighteen, Birger was regarded as incurably insane. His fate appeared to be sealed.

Then, in early 1990, his parents heard, through the work of the American speech therapist Annegret Schubert, of the therapy known as facilitated communication. This procedure begins by assuming that autistics and other people regarded as mentally disabled often do in fact have intellectual capabilities, but cannot express them verbally because of a psychological block or a motor block. To overcome such blocks, only a tiny amount of physical support is necessary: someone the affected person trusts sits at a typewriter or computer keyboard with the patient—in fact, a spelling board of letters would do—and supports his lower arm. This external aid gives the person the self-confidence and strength to press the keys with his index finger and thus express himself in writing. Many autistic people have learned language with this system. Speaking autistics who use the method are able to conquer the problem of repeating the same words over and over.

Facilitated communication was developed in 1977 by the Australian teacher Rosemary Crossley, founder of the DEAL Communication Centre in Melbourne. Crossley first used her method with people with cerebral palsy, and later extended its use to people with other disabilities. With facilitated communication, she found a key to the locked minds of these people.

The physical support is necessary initially not only to support the writer's hand and isolate the forefinger but to compensate for the weak muscle tone that many autistic people have. Moreover, the person writing gains a sense of security from the facilitator's encouraging words and gestures. As time goes on, mechanical support can be either withdrawn entirely or reduced to a hand laid on the writer's shoulder.

In the beginning, professionals regarded facilitated communication with skepticism, wondering whether the writing might not actually be the creation of the person holding the autistic person's arm. Today, although it is still controversial, facilitated communication is used all over the world, and the success rate is very high. It has helped many parents to receive news for the first time from the imprisoned minds of their autistic children. Usually such messages are desperate cries of loneliness. They also provide evidence that autistic people have mental lives of their own, lives in complete contrast to their behavior. Birger's was one such life.

THE ABYSS OPENS

The abyss into which Birger had fallen at the age of two opened up on the computer screen with a complex and bizarre linguistic beauty that took his parents' breath away. "It was like tapping a sudden spring of water," recalls Annemarie Sellin.

At first, of course, it was a laborious process. Birger typed only isolated words. Following the instructions for facilitated communication, his parents began by getting him to identify photographs and pictures, starting with members of his family, moving on to various animal species and household items, and then to factual questions about daily life. Birger answered everything accurately. On September 8, 1990, thirteen days after he began writing, he wrote for his mother: "i love you." One can hardly begin to imagine Annemarie Sellin's feelings when she read those words, after all the years of silence.

Almost every evening since then, Birger has been sitting and writing at the computer in his parents' study,

usually with his mother supporting him. With pains-
taking effort, he adds letter to letter. Every word is a new
birth. Sometimes he will have one of his attacks as he is
writing; he hits and bites himself and still goes on
writing. At first he wrote five to ten lines an evening; his
concentration would not last any longer. Now, on good
days, he fills whole pages: "ive often been scared because
people didnt know i could understand everything so they
just said everything things i wasnt meant to be hearing
. . . i would like to suggest everyone is extra sensitive
because i can hear a bit too much and see a bit too much
but my sense organs are okay its just that im afraid theres
a muddle going on inside words sentences ideas get all
torn apart and torn up and the simplest things get
wrenched out of the way they connect up in the important
real one and only other outside world a thought is really
difficult like being boxed up in the inside world."

Birger's "coming out" felt like a shattering natural phenomenon to his family. "We'd given up hope," Annemarie
Sellin says. "It's discouraging," adds her husband, "when
you've been trying for years to make contact with your
child and nothing works." When contact had finally been
made, it showed the parents that they knew nothing at all
about their son.

It turned out that Birger had not only been registering
everything going on around him over the years very precisely, but he had also been able to read and write since
he was five. As he "leafed through" all those books, he was
actually reading them. Birger's photographic memory,
which could register the absence of a single marble in a
fraction of a second, needed only a few minutes to take in
the contents of a book: after all, he had all the time in the

world to go through in his head what he had read. Only Birger knows how much he stored in that head. He has come up with scientific terms, details of the life of Galileo, the capital cities of the world, theoretical articles on research into autism, even sentences in English: "i have read many extraordinarily impressive books since my fifth year of life and i hoard all their important contents in me like precious treasures."

For almost eighteen years Birger had to stand by and see himself treated like a feebleminded toddler, and watch the crazy way he acted whether he wanted to or not, in full awareness of his state. For years he had to watch, in silence, as he was ignored and misunderstood, as people discussed things in front of him that were sure to hurt his feelings, as they prodded and pushed him at the day center to perform tasks far below his intellectual level. For years he suffered constant humiliation, without any way to work off the pain and pressure except by screaming and hitting himself. At the same time, these attacks suffered by his external self were strange and weird to him. He was left with a seriously disturbed sense of self-worth and "a fear of giving himself away," as his father puts it. "Presumably," adds Dankward Sellin, "that is why he doesn't speak, although he could." Asked about this—for he responds directly to questions on the computer—Birger wrote that he was not going to speak in the future either, "because talking is too precious and im not worth being able to talk i cant learn how because id only talk nonsense." Elsewhere, he says: "a lonely person is always replacing important experiences of poor humanity on this earth by constantly talking mostly in his lonely mind."

The loneliness overshadowing his entire life is at the

center of Birger's writing. He describes his condition as "being isolated" and "buried alive"; "i am drowning in loneliness," he complains, and he writes about "an old simple way of seeing things a going out of oneself a crate from which i am rising that would be a dream such as everyone dreams but i dont see any way out of this crate which is me even this important writing isnt enough a way out destroys my old security i am afraid of it." But "somethings will grow from walls one day that will rejoice the eye . . . there is a germ of hope in everything."

Birger regards himself, the "withoutme being from the kingdom of dark figures," with a curious mixture of despair and irony. He calls himself "idiotic totally crazy birger," a "clumsy great apeman," a "typical donkey," and "neanderthal man in person," leading "a life in a groove theres no end in sight." His life takes place "from second-class reality," from which he sends "messages from worlds below to the people of the straightforward world above." Birger writes that "our world is inaccessible and sad i want to point out that i love my own reality too it offers me protection and refuge it gives me dignity."

At the same time Birger is desperately seeking his place in real life. His mood constantly veers between hope and depression. "i dont want to be inside me anymore" is the aim he has set himself. He wants to shed his autism in any way he can ("i will murder it," he writes), to find a way into the "real confused world," the world of "people all the same," whom he would so much like to join. But "people like birger scare them and have to be isolated . . . a socalled magic power is exercised on me when i write about it and a power forces me to keep quiet about it its like a demon forcing me such a monster it keeps making me repeat things all the time to hiss do kidstuff and lead a crazy person's life its like an eternal battle." About a year later, this is how he sounds: "i receive crazy orders sour as vinegar from the heart of the strange internal festering command center responsible."

The recurring conflict between simultaneously wanting and fearing to belong to the real world is something Birger relates to other autistics as well as himself. On the one hand, he "would really like you to know what its like inside autistic children," and he asks his mother: "can you imagine what its like living in a society which keeps saying youre crazy its the absolute incarnation of such products of elementary evil theres really no way to describe it." Birger wants to help people "to recognize the internal stages of autism developing so as to get more and more people out of their boxed in lives." He explains: "as an autistic i serve other autistics as their regular spokesman" and utters a gloomy prophecy: "we will come back from swamps of silence crying out." On the other hand, he sometimes fears that he is breaking a taboo with his revelations, speaking of things that are no one else's business: "i am a real traitor," he writes suddenly, "i will talk and then survive you in eternal safety." Or: "i have so often like you wanted with an iron will to retreat into the silence and peace of our dignified and honest autistic world."

The sense that he feels he is giving himself away goes deep and is not easily overcome. Writing has not just made it possible for Birger to articulate his life; at the same time it has reached into his laboriously constructed security system. "most of all i would like to weep like socalled important people but its no good it is as if a stone being is holding me a prisoner and it thinks sorrow is a security risk it is like an iron ring around my chest." He sees this world as very strange: "our wonderful island of the plundering horrible master race . . . i dont fit into this crazy cowardly horrible society this assortment of steely ace performers it all feels wrong." Birger reacted to the outbreak of the Gulf War with horror, for instance, and took part in an antiwar demonstration. Details do not escape his hypersensitive notice either, including hostile or cold glances from people in the street: "a lonely and mute person depends on encouragement . . . a loving look does wonders without words . . . once in the subway i saw a woman looking at me kindly i often think of it i like to believe in it and i won't forget it but many looks are hard to bear and bring dreadful suffering with them."

Irony helps him to arm himself against his feelings of inferiority and isolation. "an outcast is sorry to seem so silly to those wellbehaved very clever knowalls," Birger wrote one day after our first meeting, apologizing for the tantrum he had in front of me. When a psychologist acquaintance of his parents who was fascinated by his writing tried to reach out to him, he wrote ironically: "now it looks as if i am going to be enormously important how will the importance suit my socalled real inner soul just think of the way people take trouble for someone like me its the doing of a steely person like [the name followed] eager for action she was at the institution and wanted to talk to someone uncommon like me." Birger also casts a sardonic eye on the center for young autistics (which in fact he likes very much). He calls the center a "really wayout what they call a madhouse its just great im sure those important amazingly stuckup people arent good for much anyway but those conceited great crazy brutes of teachers certainly arent . . . the crazy talk of the real important teachers gets on the nerves of an envious birger a bit . . . i seize the first socalled opportunity to interrupt them and i scream bloody murder."

In spite of all his doubts and misgivings about the loss of security he is risking, Birger seems to be fully aware of the consequences of his self-therapy. He is fighting his autism at immense internal cost. A reader who follows the development of his thinking will understand that. (I have been quoting here arbitrarily, not in chronological order.) Birger is trying both to work out the causes and idiosyncrasies of his disability and to solve the problem of how his environment functions, which to his mind is just as large a problem. He asks himself, for instance: "but how can a person really know what a sensible reason is how can a person know how things work if he is shut out of society and doesnt know important words properly." He answers: "all on his own he puts together wonderful explanations for himself totally crazy rough hewn answers buckets full of garbage."

It is especially in his correspondence with the Berlin developmental psychologist Gisela Ulmann (she appears in his writing as "rightthinking chosen gisela") that Birger tries to find answers to "questions why" and puzzle out the mysteries of normal life. "right now i am trying to get a realistic grasp of small things but i dont see how i can really check up on it." His progress, measured by his relatively short "writing period," has been enormous. And yet Birger is still severely autistic. "without language i am a poor madman and i can write only with the help of another person which is very humiliating and i am ashamed of it," he admits in a letter.

Outwardly, Birger seems much the same as he was when

I first met him. He might be described as intellectually adult but emotionally and socially still a child. "It's difficult to understand," says a staff member at his center. "He can read and write but he acts like a madman." He still suffers his screaming fits and tantrums, and they have become even harder to predict, partly in reaction to being treated with condescension, partly as they express a mysterious but deep-seated anger over the irrevocable loss of the security of his mute childhood years. To him, the future may seem uncertain and menacing: "fear comes over me thats all first i have a funny feeling in my stomach then the anxiety comes up on the sly to attack my whole body like a cunning beast." Then he cannot help screaming, because "a poor what they call birger cant get the fear out of his mind."

His stereotypical behavior used to help him suppress feelings of anxiety: "one anxiety i suffer from most of all is how to survive a day . . . i for my part protect against the icy times of day by setting up a socalled steely important list of questions an idiot system as it were running away from anxiety." Birger's marbles, representing to him a world full of symbolism, are part of this "idiots system." They convey "ideas from the world of people without any social value and its also a world of asocial people its the indefinable product of mankind." Letting marbles run through his fingers is "a stereotypy i repeat when i am really in a rage showing visibly what loneliness does invisibly." Here again, Birger retains his remarkable sense of humor. "the autistics view of life," he writes, "is like a ship sinking and making up nonsense to keep from noticing i am captain of this ship and my nonsense is real hardthinking how to opt out of it size."

By now, Birger has ventured so far out of his autistic cage that stereotypy has lost its power, and he cannot return to it. The price for such progress is an increase in his internal restlessness—he calls the phenomenon "great depths of restless force . . . as long as i can remember the restlessness has been there a force like no one can imagine it almost makes me crazy . . . when i was even smaller my stereotypical behavior was a little help." But now, explains Birger, "these mechanisms dont work so well any more that is why ive been screaming so much recently. . . . i cant live in peace and quiet with this anxiety i must scream anxiety gives the boxed in feelings the upper hand and they stifle me i am a slave to the vast force of anxiety."

Despite the relapses and setbacks, Birger's parents and his therapist, Margard Breinlinger, see a clear improvement in his behavior since he began writing, and particularly since the tremendous reaction to the publication of his work in the German press. But he did seem to go through a severe crisis in the spring of 1991. During this time he hardly wrote at all, and his parents feared he might fall completely silent again. His therapist explains the condition by saying that Birger had become "totally confused" by coming out. But he picked himself up and began writing again. He has been using a portable notebook computer for short daily communications. In the summer of 1992 he even attended a lecture at Berlin's Free University. Birger had repeatedly made it known that he was interested in studying linguistics (choosing as a specialty the love poetry of the Renaissance). In the fall of that year he attended two lectures on psychology, but he was too strained by the experience to try it again. Sitting through a lecture was an enormous effort for him, but Birger is bent on proving himself able to do things that others do. He has also agreed to let the French director Jamila Chauvet make a film about his life.

Birger expresses the hope that *I Don't Want to Be Inside Me Anymore* will not be a "trashy book just a really thoughtprovoking book in a good form from which you can see i want to take part in real wide life."

THE WRITINGS

Birger's writing is his only means of expression. It is a mixture of personal and family communications, descriptions of his condition, accounts like those in a diary, poems, letters, and reflections on various subjects. From the start, Birger's parents kept everything their son wrote—hardly surprising in view of the dramatic turning point the beginning of his "writing period" meant for the family.

To keep the book's length reasonable and its content useful, I have decided to include here only a selection from this material. I have chosen pieces that reveal what Birger has to say about his autism or that seem to me to have literary value because of his unique outlook on the world and the directness of his expression. Another criterion was to show the course of his development, something that should be of particular interest to psychologists, therapists, and parents of autistic children. The texts are arranged in chronological order, not by subject. His first attempts may not seem to make much sense, but they clearly illustrate the difficulties Birger had to confront at the beginning.

Not least, I wanted to present Birger's writing in a form

that would require a minimum of footnoted explanations. This proved particularly difficult with Birger's correspondence. There did not seem to me much point in printing other people's letters to Birger as well as his replies, and I think those replies will make it clear what they are about. I have resorted to footnotes when people or events really need explaining. When Birger was replying directly to questions from his parents, those questions are printed here as well, in capital letters.

Each excerpt is followed by the date when it was written. When the time between writings stretches over a long period, it does not mean that Birger wrote nothing during that time—he writes almost every day—but just that those passages were not selected for the book. Apart from his letters, all direct address is to his parents.

Writing gets Birger very excited. When this state of excitement rises to a certain level, his writing hand may not be entirely under his control. Sometimes he also suffers attacks while he is writing, which lead to typing errors and incomplete words. At Birger's request I have corrected such mistakes. The only exceptions are the writings from the first few weeks (up to December 10, 1990), which are also intended to illustrate his early difficulties. To show how an attack of screaming affects the appearance of the writing, see page 158. Apart from the effects of his emotional state on his writing, Birger has an excellent command of spelling and grammar. As soon as he began writing for longer periods, he made hardly any typing errors. Now and then, however, there are missing parts of speech, or passages of the German in the wrong grammatical case. As a rule this is because, in his excitement, Birger began a sentence one way and finished it another. I have not corrected such passages. The absence of capital letters (Birger types with one finger) also reflects the original—a more striking absence in German, in which all nouns have initial capital letters—and so does the lack of punctuation marks.

The selection here ends in 1992. Birger is still writing.

Michael Klonovsky
Munich, 1993

AUGUST

---

abcdefghijklmnopqrstuvwxyz
birger papa jonasmama

8.27.90

zhietypahwbb
grandma granddad ffaammily
jonas paapa birger mama yebml

8.28.90

746103289julikasa
vvolkkhard
clim tree yes

8.29.90

carr grandpa and grandma jonas tookit packet
pockets wettblgghnukoa
father mother brotther mmölln
peepl
stopnow owllglass

8.30.90

37

js yes
ttyes
ppapa
beaverr
ererrrest st bedkkk
no

8.31.90

I don't want to be inside me anymore

SEPTEMBER

———

yes
sdofg
dog
wollllf
flamigo
cow
bisonn
vvulture
mmama
jonas
birger
waattter sea
beach
ppapa
ccamera
hooold hand
uuuuuuuuuuuuuuuuuuuuuuuuuuuuuu
no more
go to sleep

9.3.90

biirger jonas ugzret sword skin
feeear eyepattch hziuzfz pirate
jonas franzmax mama bench we ssit
stork bison wolf sstp stop

9.4.90

xenia bernd birger
drinks juice
wolfgang talk
ridebike i like ridridingbike
yes i want to stop

9.5.90

bathhroom bath jonas birger david
monkey baaby cave dog kangarooh baby
elephant climb wolff bbear
im going to stop

9.6.90

duuck duck
packet nest eggs
mask basket caaamel camel
hedgehog cucumber grass
i would like tosstop to sstop

9.7.90

I don't want to be inside me anymore

packet telephone lamp arm pen
car ball apple cow foot bed traffic light
scissors locomotive ladder spooon
i dont i want tto stop
i love youyes

9.8.90

up laugh 1 2 323 4 5 6 7 88 9 10m 11 12 13 14 15 16 17
18 19 20 21 212 23 24
255 26 27
to down

9.9.90

beeans n6
leaf 7
5 flowers
i wwant ssstop

9.12.90

3 flowers
shells5
3 nail screw
starfish 5
2 buttons
7leaf leaves
5flowwers 9 red blue yellow5
5 bbutterfly
i sstopp id like to
gdown
to down
smell with nose

9.13.90

ggratzuvggh
uyyfu.pgxf
sayos
yes yes sojhffcdzrarsss
soyasaucelkio
okooklmk
karf
. . . hhh
tdooggf
yes
kidstuff
tgjkgfdggfg

9.14.90

I don't want to be inside me anymore

yes
to goo salofd
to cook spaghetti meellonnn
melone cheese i to ibbooliflholp
potato
mmembmgjhb
i want to stop

9.15.90

papa iekvuxct
a bc d re f g hh ij k l m n o p q r s t u v w x y z

9.16.90

2 and 3 = 5
go to slleep

9.17.90

eagle
the eagle iss a bird of prey[*]
nomore

9.18.90

[*]The sentences from "the eagle iss a bird of prey" to "i am playing with with building blockss" were dictated to Birger.

there are 4 ccandles burning onn the advent wrreath
not write any more

9.19.90

yes
on the first day in advent birger and jonas get a
gingerbread house
write more
car evening
im going to sstop

9.20.90

ii stoopp

9.21.90

the astronaut fflies in space
apaau
stop

9.22.90

I don't want to be inside me anymore

birger
will bake cakes in the bakery
i want to hvv have quiet

9.23.90

i am playing with with
building blockss
have anegg
gasys
have peace
a phaase
ppp
im sad because i cant tallk yyet

9.24.90

please to bedd

9.25.90

im going toslee sleep
going to sleep

9.26.90

iii donnt want
to write sowhat

9.27.90

can i eat whats
on all the plates

9.29.90

yes
i dont
i mu uust sooo
yes
alrarat
yy
yourenot any garbazucket
garbage buucket

9.30.90

OCTOBER

———

yes
illl
yyy
dont wannt to write today

10.1.90

imm a hobljl
im a gorri
gorribte
rrrrinn
horink
horrible person

10.16.90

i wannt to go home
can hagg
simpply habv good time
you shl should
like firdud more since everyone ss
says youre so kind
itss the sas sadhc
saysso letssa
sd begin t GETTING BETTER Fs sosf
wo so t ta take care
b but biirger can
t get anywhere without love
all a ft
ut yt uts just vr very
very very dear aw aaberb barsr af
area say
asay that you loveme
ss say ay that you all jonas too and dannkward adw aswell
all i liiike specially anne adc
whenyou sclded
scold bsys bahs soals

10.22.90

NOVEMBER

---

today was letsay kindof
a and not act the way
i llike it because im different from other people
but id rather not be that way
other people say im handicapped

11.4.90

cc can i call people crazt crazy so
i dont have to liike
nobody liket crrraxy people

11.9.90

you must help me to talk
you mh must gol hold my arm
ththe question is will we be able to talk clearly enough
only when we are really
a all died dead get our shpe of being
the way we want it
thats why i often wish i was dead
because im alone in my loneliness

11.24.90

I don't want to be inside me anymore

you mustnt scold but today
you were very pattient i dont fit into the widde world atall
   because im afraid im
just afraid of
ordinary things that seem as hala harmless
as buildings
well they seem threatening to me im always scared
but today it was specially bad becc
be cause you shouted at me like that today i couldnt
do up my coat
it bothered me so much bb
its not really so bad
then it gets bad when im scared i think thats crazy but
   once i couldnt find my bead*
zannd 1 but nothing bad happened
wh which is why im stupid when im scared its ve ry
stupid when
okay so you cnn can laugh when
i scream out loud but yyou did tht that long before i
could talk

11.25.90

---

*One of his marbles.

51

i will tell you all about it when i can write better i dont
  have enough skill id like to be much
better i liked being alone with jonas today more than i
  ssometimes do thats your fault just
think of the years without him i need say no more or cant
  you remember them any more jonas
is a nice boy birger is nicer than he is
not a bad boy particularly yesterday i couldnt write when
  you were cross like that
im not cross with you but birger is so sensitive that he
  cant
stand anything that disturbs him

11.29.90

DECEMBER

---

im no notthing nothing atall

12.9.90

on saturday dankward couldnt write much with me
    because he was sad because you were sick
he always works very hard but he is the nicest lets say the
    dearest father
yesterday he was lets say not such fun but today he was
    lets say funny

12.10.90

solomon was a wise king i know it all only i cant say it in fact its only in writing i can say things at speed i mean lets say fast i can say things that scare people but i dont do that ive often been scared because people didnt know i understand everything so they just said everything i wasnt supposed to be hearing i only liked being at those parties in the world at the time but otherwise i thought up all kinds of things so i could get out of that way of being the silliest idea was when i thought it could all be switched off now i dont need those methods any more because now i can write so thats that i never said so much before as i did today but now its a pity its over

12.13.90

astronomy is about the stars but i dont believe in the stars because it isnt likely that constellations could give advice lets say it can be proved that the earth is only lets say a structure in space

12.14.90

g.* tells me all sorts of things ive known for ages yesterday
she explained how the potato is a fruit of the earth which
any fool knows jonas is right all animals are clever because
they know what they need to live on jonas is so straightforward he is always a pleasure to be with even when youre
cross with him the fact is i lets say i like it but we are
so often upset for trivial reasons i want everything to be
specially good on sunday then everything will be okay
again i dont need presents better be friendly than have lots
of presents

12.15.90

achim† was lets say asocial yes that word is taken out say
what you like it still makes no sense what kind of sense
would it make the fact is achim was very social asocial if
you are explaining things about adaptation we all have to
keep adapting to a social system but almost everything we
actually do is a kind of adaptation darwin was the first
person to work on that subject which as you might expect
he lets say deduced from his ideas that social species are
inherited its a fact but the species say something about the
social nature of races seeds are crossed

12.17.90

*A woman who teaches in the Center for Young Autistics.
†A case helper in the center with whom Birger has a particularly close
relationship.

55

you ought to give yourself more rest the fact is you work very hard its really too much the way you work so hard its bad the way youre always at it lets say like a workhorse be a little more settled i am looking for the cursor its so ingenious im amazed the way it functions i am interested to see how it works

12.18.90

if we are going to be damned for our sins then i think belief is okay as you say there must be a god who thinks we are all very precious but who is going to save me will this salvation come only after death who will we be after we rise again i really enjoy writing i have so many questions

12.19.90

when i wanted to say things totally lets say important facts spoke very clearly out of me they were facts about the world and the earth these are things that i wont lets say talk about till later when a good day comes its lets say like another spirit speaking to me

12.22.90

i do want you to know what its like inside autistic children without touching on the writing we are lets say so scared its a fear like no other can you imagine what its like living in a social system that is always saying youre crazy it embodies such products of elementary evil that theres no way to describe it knowing about these things shows us that our system cant be right i want everyone to know that autistic children arent stupid the way people often think im not a real person without the writing because its the only means of expression i have and its the only way of showing how i think and i do it too but its still very difficult i find it very exhausting

12.23.90

i want something which i just cant learn from any creature in this world im bursting with restlessness and impatience i would so much like to find my way out of my isolated life out of decadent ways of behaving which i use like armor i feel only frustration day in day out without hope in this life of ever being lifted out or wiped out of this hopeless isolation or having it wiped out i cant make a just a little socalled tiny problem out of the very weighty lets say serious facts of isolation the fact is it is technically impossible its almost sure not to succeed

12.25.90

i dont know whose patience is greater yours or a computers but the computers isnt genuine while on the other hand yours is almost entirely straightforward the fact is i could already write and even do arithmetic when i was almost five but nobody noticed because i was so chaotic but i was only that way because i was afraid of people its just because i wasnt able to talk i found reading so easy and so i looked in lets say important books for everything i could find the books were all in that socalled room in that lets say study in kreuzberg but later there were also books from the study in lots of real apartments where we lived today i do it all by myself

12.26.90

I don't want to be inside me anymore

madrid is the capital of portugal
surinam is the capital of tanzania*
the fact that i am not naming any more capitals means
that i have to learn to answer questions thoroughly first no
schoolboy ought to answer that way i would like to go to a
real school and learn like other children first we will keep
coming across socalled satirical people then they will realize that i am clever too and can do everything they want
now i am still often rather hesitant but it will be quite different in school and i will act like any other child there and
learn things too i would also learn how to behave to people
who actually cure lonely growing up people of autistic agitation to express a hope its true there are no stupid autistics
there is no way out without hope anyone can see that

12.28.90

---

*When his parents asked what he had been reading during the silent years,
Birger answered (on the keyboard) that he knew, for instance, all the capital
cities of the world. After giving these two wrong answers, he was fired up,
and the next day he gave the capitals without a single mistake. Some of his
answers are printed in subsequent texts.

lisbon madrid dar es salaam panamaribo
yes i am glad but i can see all that about school is ridiculous because i am a restless spirit i show no obvious understanding if a miracle happened lets say this restless spirit
became calmer articulated better so that everyone could
understand what he was saying the way speaking people
easily understand each other then all the same its a fact it
would be too difficult for me but i havent entirely given up
that hope

12.29.90

1991

JANUARY

i dont want to do sums because i am too big i am big and
    clever and handicapped
i am a sad case
they tied me down in the hospital* at night
didnt you like coming to see me every day then
anyway i dont want to be handicapped

1.7.91

*Birger is referring to his stay in the Wiesengrund children's hospital (see the
introduction).

tirana no idea Andorra del ville
yes i do know all the cities so leave me alone sofia
today i really want to tell you what its like at school in the
center at tonukohass i want to leave that word it means
dont get worked up in the no additions language which is a
language for all socalled stupid people i invented it there is
also a personal grammar for this language riokeea means
the braid of hair is long i was unhappy today because the
writing still wouldnt work okay with achim* i am probably too uncertain whenever it gets really serious thats when
you switch off its only when there is no prospect of effective ways you come down like a raging fury on an oasis
when i am totally agitated it is terrible yesterday evening i
wrote for the first time with dankward the way i do with
you it was really wonderful

1.8.91

personally i would like to attend a course for able colleagues all idiots i even know english but not very much
say a word and i will say it in english *middle book* that was
much too easy for me *i am the greatest i am the also best of the
world* yes i have read everything and very fast i even read
scientific books very quickly and i make up so much myself
even stories and poems

1.9.91

---

*At first facilitated communication would work for Birger only with his
parents and his personal case helper, Tycho Nickel. He wrote only a few
isolated words with the support of Achim, the case helper from the center.

I don't want to be inside me anymore

*town car newspaper ok police railstation lion**
beside the wall under cress grief i dont want to write any
    more

1.10.91

vaduz
i am so sad because it doesnt work so well on my own
i cant write it down because it is so horrible
i am thinking of destroying everything that wasnt
    destroyed in the ice age

1.11.91

luxemburg valletta monaco
dont you like the way i would lets say like to kill saddam
hussein because he is beginning a war achim ought to know
that i don't like the war there either life would be hell without writing achim ought to know everything about me i
will only be able to live away from home when i have
learned how to write by myself thats a fact because otherwise everyone will say you are writing the things i write

1.12.91

*Birger is translating words given by his mother in German into English.

65

amsterdam oslo warshawa warsaw
today i am going to tell a story once upon a time in a
lonely little town there lived a wonderful young woman
she was very sad because she was so alone she was a poor
widow and had nobody in the world but along came
another man and married her on the spot and they lived a
loving poor life so that they didnt mind anything in the
world as they were sitting there along came a darkness
from the atmosphere and the air turned dreadfully sticky
so that no one dared to breathe any more its a fact they all
died but i will go on with this story tomorrow because it
is much too long

1.13.91

i will tell some more of that story
when the darkness scared people they saw nothing after
that everything was wrapped in darkness but there were
more and more people wandering around in the streets if
an accident happened no one could help anyone else but if
a like massive disaster i mean a gigantic misfortune happened then they got in a panic many of them were really
dead there wasnt any house where nothing happened they
were all gone underground for socalled security reasons unfortunately water came bubbling up from the depths and a
lot of people were drowned and there were fabulous appari-
tions over the earth too which scared the rest of them sav-
age pterodactyls attacked the globe its a fact that very large
species from primeval times appeared just like it said in the
bible

1.15.91

66

I don't want to be inside me anymore

i dont find children a strain children are so spontaneous they understand much more than adults children actually have more sensitive feelings than adults i am sure a lot goes wrong in school but children get over that as i noticed with our jonas yesterday it didnt worry me at all that tycho was there it is important for tycho that i tell him what i want to experience but i cant say it because in fact i have no idea about the socalled real fun things there are for lets say young people i would like to find out what its like in a disco because i think that sounds very exciting

1.18.91

no one talks worse nonsense thats to say it is less foolish than jaksson* who is a lets say pop singer he is so exciting i saw him on television he was singing a song about keasatsad yes that means the world is made for you and not for soldiers we mustnt allow everything on earth to be bombed when i heard that strong song sung fast in haste i had an ejaculation for the first time ive been lets say a fan of jakssons ever since then

1.19.91

*The singer Michael Jackson.

67

this is about astronomy there was galilei he discovered
    scientific methods he lived from 1564 to 1642
i want to tell you all about things again but its so difficult
    thats why i was such bad company
i couldnt find a word

                                                        1.24.91

i want to adopt you
yes it always bothers me when other people help me write
                                                        1.27.91

birger seems quiet but he isnt handicapped because he can
    show feelings
                                                        1.31.91

FEBRUARY

———

dont you like me being really sad when theres a bead missing i am so disappointed because everyone doubts whether i write all this by myself the people in the school center said so and i even heard some teacher in the socalled study room and there was a psychologist there too i was in the next room and i could hear everything

2.6.91

beads are almost as important as a real valuable working method i use them to work on personal theories i even get real knowledge its about knowledge from the world of the dasra that means people without any social value to their lives and its a world which includes asocial types its the indefinable waste matter of humanity

2.7.91

so far as i am aware even psychologists know lets say
hardly anything essential i am not exaggerating and achim
says that without studying people guess so to speak what
young autistics want the most important microorganisms
are singlecelled creatures in water plankton is lets say
organisms floating but not moving in water they move
among other algae theres diatoms and conjugata and
bluegreen algae

2.14.91

chemistry is exciting but id rather do biology this
semester* but dont worry i think i will soon be enjoying a
lot of other subjects

2.16.91

amoebas are lets say water creatures in micro-organic life
the living creatures which move about swimming are
called nekton our dankward knows a lot about the first
great step forward which brought forth real life it is called
cell division

2.18.91

---

*Birger's parents are asking him questions on various academic subjects to find
out what he has read.

the way you keep talking on and on i suffer the torments
of hell i am afraid you are seeing it all wrong you have no
idea about life in total isolation its worse than a prison or
what they call solitary confinement i am drowning in
loneliness

2.20.91

you dont notice very much or you would know how
important it is for me to have a person always close to me
firmly linked to my humble self like you

2.24.91

MARCH

———

i dont want to be inside me anymore
i have eyes and i can see so i have been terribly scared and
    so i didnt want to say any more about that
i was afraid of the end of the road and the end of humanity

3.7.91

i dont fit into this crazy cowardly horrible society it is so
weird this selection of strong ace performers

3.9.91

i cant say anything sensible without staying unrecognized
    its all lies

3.14.91

I don't want to be inside me anymore

i am not talking so much these days
because i am feeling sad again these days

3.17.91

being clever as a clever trick and as lets say a permanent
way of looking at things shows a weak character

3.22.91

APRIL

———

talking is something very important to me it is a device
for making dead people come alive again and for crazy
lonely people it replaces their social disorientation

4.22.91

when i wanted to have a steely heart without being made
of stone i was going a little too fast a totally soft creature
is one without any stone

4.25.91

red rich shining sun on the horizon this is a poem i have
made up myself a poem which is close to my heart

4.28.91

MAY

———

i so often get the letters wrong without help but when
someone is holding on properly it all goes easily this is
like a desolate image the fact is even a word can be very
eventful it can stir you right up

5.16.91

only beings of raging knowing wisdom will work wonders
he will simply learn how with what torment a lonely
being arises from this earth he makes his lonely way on
again and again there are desolate wonders
neither you nor i will know who it is

5.27.91

if you give everyone lessons in the technique of this strong method of writing which is sure to succeed* the way annegret† taught you i think in a way that would be silly because there are people who are too stupid for the technique

5.29.91

and an adversary will rise from the sea wearing very strong iron chains an arsenal of weapons dripping ore like fire will rise from the deep from his chosen people he will first pick a chosen arsenal of socalled iron archangels the chosen ones will replace the first ace performers
all this is out of the bible

5.31.91

---

*After the method had proved successful with her son, Annemarie Sellin began giving seminars on facilitated communication all over Germany, using Birger's writings as illustrative material.

†Annegret Schubert, an American speech therapist, brought the facilitated communication method to Germany.

JUNE

---

birger is an able backward person
even a dimmer person would remember her* i know
perfectly well who she is she is the most effective lets say
the fact is most effective therapist i first had in wonderful
sponholz street and she will never be blotted out of my
memory

6.3.91

i would very much like to tell our disorientated teachers
that they ought to talk like sensible beings and not talk
nonsense

6.5.91

today i feel lonely and bad and a lonely person is one
thinking without tumult he is a steely dead person and is
always superfluous in this world even with an arsenal of
firstclass fabulous people anxious to do something trying
to amuse him

6.7.91

*Birger's first therapist, Margard Breinlinger, who is now treating him again.

the one and only eager iron lonely man wants to write a first and only iron precious thought a poem

6.13.91

it is so sad for me that nobody understands me but it is important for a lot of people to understand me a bit but achim does not understand me enough and the others dont take any trouble with a person like me any more its enough to drive one to despair

6.19.91

i dont perceive experience properly

6.20.91

I don't want to be inside me anymore

it is certainly a simply enormous strain telling other
    people what being isolated all the time is like
it would probably be rather too difficult for a person like
    wonderful important birger
but it is good that our proficient first person is writing to
    our dear proficient second person
the first proficient person is denise*
our dear first person was really totally sweet
she is such a fine example of autistic misery that you are
    lets say all saying today that she is the dregs of
    humanity
yet she is very very experienced and clever

6.22.91

---

*An autistic girl four years younger than Birger who attended the day center
with him and who is also writing by means of facilitated communication.
Birger calls her the first and himself the second because at the center they
were both considered to be on the lowest educational level.

do you really know how deep-rooted anxiety can be in an
    individual
the way it eats away an individual
the way it works personally on a single person at the
    collapse of the first agonizing words
it is like total perception
the meadows will be green the sun will certainly be
    shining brightly if the anxiety goes away
for just a minute
it is kind of an incredible way to improve values a simple
    momentary glance into eternity
a totally monstrous light in total darkness

6.24.91

like everything else a date happens to be a matter of
    rotating events
its a fact time serves the purpose of a little of the total
    eternal centrifugal onedimensional
framework in which we humans live

6.29.91

I don't want to be inside me anymore

the way one of your sons upset you today will certainly
  never ever happen again
if you are going to react like that another time without
  good reason then a state of agitation is really important
  and it is none of my doing so you will see there is no
  point getting so obviously upset
i thought our jonas was lost you see*

6.30.91

*Birger's brother, Jonas, had gone home on his own from a summer party in the neighborhood where the family lives. When he suddenly realized that Jonas was missing, Birger lost control completely and hit himself until he bled.

JULY

―――――

would like to find sequences which dont reflect any real
    reality

7.3.91

its a fact i wanted to find my own way home[*]
first i went by subway to the crooked lanke
and various subways i knew the avus was further on
its so hard to find your way
it was probably chance
it was on my way
it was only afterwards everything got difficult
the fact is it was very hard to find the way home
really it was quite fun but very very agitating
but it was lets say the only way i knew it was so bad i will
    never do it again
lets say east west homes always best ·

7.7.91

[*]On July 7, Birger ran away from home for the third (and so far the last) time.
At four in the afternoon he suddenly disappeared, leaving the front door open.
He went on public transport over half of Berlin, with his parents and the
police looking for him. Just before midnight the police picked him up on the
Berlin urban freeway (the Avus). That evening and the next he gave an
account of his experiences.

I don't want to be inside me anymore

i am learning really valuable things like what a dangerous
   adventure is like
i will do it again but only when its okay
that means first when the kidstuff writing works properly
   and second when our fabulous jonas
is bigger and not so worried about our fabulous birger
it upsets a person who can talk when he is worried about
   someone
in the first place i am a little sorry about you but not very
   much in the second place i need
to be independent
it gets me so worked up when its dangerous
but it isnt as bad as the anxiety otherwise it is much
   simpler to run away than being shut up
i am shut up even at home and i can only go out when you
   want and never when i want so
how come you are talking about shutting me up when i
   always am anyway
dont talk about the freeway
it upsets me so much because it was so horrible
i climbed over the fence that is standing there and i
   balanced on it

7.8.91

whatever happens i want to learn to write properly because
    it is the way to independence
first i was very scared then it was a lot of fun
really i would rather say something important if thats
    okay there are things a person like
birger thinks in the loneliness because this world ought to
    know them its like being buried
alive the loneliness of an autistic is like a great clod of
    earth weighing down the soul

7.12.91

dont get upset if you find im gone
i always come back again okay
i will never run away into the wide world again not before
    its agreed i know enough
it is possible for an odd person like me to get to be
    independent through your crazy training system
well i was so restless because the egyptian painting really
    takes it out of me*

7.14.91

*Birger had been to the Pergamon Museum with his family.

I don't want to be inside me anymore

i think i get really anxious like today for no reason
suddenly the fear is just there and then it goes again
   without any internal reason
i am working on living without ideals and without anxiety
these are my own internal aims

7.19.91

most of all i would like to weep like socalled important
people but its no good it is as if a stone being is holding
me prisoner and it thinks sorrow is a security risk it is like
an iron ring around my chest

7.24.91

how does an important citizen of the world learn to find
the wide expanses if hes never been where he wants to go

7.26.91

AUGUST

———

lets go to czechoslovakia again some day
it was fantastic
how come dankward thinks the trip totally dissolved the
   insanity and resistance of a person like me
he knows himself thats not right
how else would i work through an experience
it is simply the agitation of not being able to reply to
   talking people
and i will never learn to talk properly
because kind of first of all
i talk obvious nonsense totally silly stuff because talking is
   too valuable
because im not worth being able to talk
the fact is i can never talk
because i am too bad in my inner reality and the fact is i
   cant learn it because i would simply talk nonsense i
   know i would talk total nonsense so do the other
   autistic people they annoy others with constant
   repetition and saying silly things
i could only talk the way i write if the autism was gone
   and that wont work because there isnt any cure
it is a disturbance which cant ever be properly described

I don't want to be inside me anymore

its cutting off a person from his first simple experiences
  like essential important experiences
for instance weeping
just weeping without feeling angry beforehand and
  laughing the way children laugh

8.11.91

yes i want to tell an iron story
it is about an iron old man* wise but not very rich he
  wanted to make nonsense visible by
really making serious invisible words visible and making
  obvious nonsense invisible
a real grandpa never dies
he goes on living in my heart like before
and i will never forget him
he was an important wise person to me
he is calm and relaxed and he worked out the words just
  the way they ought to be
i love him very much

8.13.91

*Birger is writing about his dying grandfather (he died on September 19, 1991).

loneliness iron will and important unusual experiences
  give the wise person important inspiration
an iron will plagues a creature it works itself out mental
guidelines the person who accepts the mental guidelines
learns from inspiration how a lonely inspired person
becomes in my opinion sees the chosen host of the lonely
like our really lonely idiot stupid birger that means birger

8.16.91

a wise person is one who makes the right decisions in a
  difficult situation like grandpa when he left the hospital
he wants to leave this life and go down into the next life in
  loving surroundings
he personally will experience what hes preached to everyone and rise again and receive eternal life from the safe
hand which we have seized have grasped

8.18.91

i dont even cry properly to weep out an unspeakable huge
lonely wedge inside me weep out a whole existence would
be the only personal comfort

8.19.91

i create real chaos like a volcano a strong effective will is
enough to quench it there is a surging hasty spirit working
eagerly in me trying to keep the unripe fruits of a person
like knowing lonely genuine steely birger from ripening i
want to stop the yield is too poor

8.20.91

how can you know how important a really deep experience of god is for me i experience only earthly inadequacies total frankness is important i am so very keen to have an important idea again and again ideas are smothered and come to nothing

8.21.91

now it looks as if i am going to be enormously important how will the importance suit my socalled real inner soul just think of the way people take trouble for someone like me its the doing of a steely person like w.* eager for action she was at the institution and wanted to talk to someone uncommon like me

8.22.91

brutal fools strong officious people ought not to be given any opportunity of governing luckily the justified the really fair and right opposition of the people brought down the ringleaders[†]

8.23.91

---

*A psychologist acquainted with Birger's parents.
[†]Birger is referring to the attempted coup of August 1991 in Moscow.

a real lonely person judges wrong when he goes out among people he simply doesnt understand their ways a lonely person is a real solitary a strong loner longs secretly for the important company of the other steely cowards

8.27.91

how come i always have so many lonely hours i am lonely
    everywhere how come
it is always so difficult to say anything on a subject
like about my loneliness the whole story so often does no
    good even does harm because i
get really really lonely
if our tycho will be patient a poor chaotic person can do
    just about anything i thought the idea
of sending a lonely person to school* was quite good

8.28.91

how is a person fixated on sweet things to hold out to
    carry through an important personal decision
a proper way out would be for me to compete with you
we drink by the bucketful like real primeval animals how
    else do we overcome the addiction
an important idea the poems of an important man steely
    rilke†

8.30.91

---

*Birger attends a school for the educationally handicapped once a week, with his case helper.
†The poet Rainer Maria Rilke.

90

I don't want to be inside me anymore

SEPTEMBER

---

but iron will isnt enough to destroy addiction i will really
   only be free a person like me will change the lonely girl
   will be surprised to see how this judgment on me a
   steely socalled really stupid person goes
the lonely girl is a socalled crazy girl* who came to the one
   and only school center today
everyone there is lonely
simply every autistic is lonely
it does very lonely really severe damage
when they talk properly
these lonely people are so set in their ways
they hide their loneliness
enduring isolation resolutely is difficult
but strange to say you get used to it
in the first place the lonely girl has no real important
   confused name how could she get a name
but today she will be much lonelier than me
this poor crazy girl whom lonely rich really stupid birger
   quietly loves

9.9.91

*Xenia, a speaking autistic, three years younger than Birger, who had just
come to the institution.

91

it is difficult for me iron birger to be as happy as today
its like a really proper adventure
always trust me
i feel this sincere trust as a spring which gives important
    socalled earthly energy

9.15.91

a poor person gets agitated over a real lonely man so you
    get agitated because birger lets you guess everything
    but doesnt tell you details
he talks only when he wants and says only what he wants
so why do you ask an obvious siberian polar bear like
    important birger questions
someone like that someone steely in loneliness would
    never put questions to you

9.28.91

the really rough and ready division like mealtimes was
    idiotic once its a fact there was no meal because we had
    missed out on the norms
food always fills a single animal lonely person
like others with a happy conception
a lonely person is crazily properly busily eager to is really
    addicted to keeping to the right times he does it just
    compulsively

9.29.91

I don't want to be inside me anymore

simple as it sounds a cure everyone could surely recognize
   could judicially prove is possible
a thought which i think incredible it will work
unfortunately simply believing it is not enough
simply believing it means looking for ways out too

9.30.91

OCTOBER

——

once i went rigid with fear unintentionally because i
    thought dripping waterdrops were living creatures
it was only when i looked more closely i saw they were
    waterdrops
sometimes i still get illusions like that
but they dont scare me as much as they used to

10.4.91

not everyone is right for it* working with support really
   properly perseveringly so that i get the feeling i can
   speak dependently but freely
i dont think we will find the remnants of such a sure
   persevering freedom of thought in very many lonely
   autistic people
collected thoughts totally dormant tremble with cold
   when they make their way to the outside light of earth
they are so sensitive and shy but they give other people an
   impression of the unusual world of the lonely
if i werent writing my lonely thoughts would die out so
   would my very personal stories they would simply die
but i can write it all down so that nothing can simply die
   but will live on
i will write properly as soon as the independent writing
   looks like no one can think oh nonsense he isnt writing
   alone at all it is the person supporting his arm
they are trying to discourage me again the way they did
   before discouraging me with vexatious doubts
some of the teachers say these things in the school center

10.5.91

*For facilitated communication.

how come birger is so alone again
he changes too slowly
nobody notices it
unfortunately no one appreciates how difficult it is to turn
    asocial into social behavior
resolutely turn nonsense into sense
changing takes more energy than you really understand
people expect it to take place any time
but nobody asks how difficult it is
i am a coward i am keen to be really successful some time

10.6.91

watch out when your really important crazy birger talks
    calmly
only then will i say something directly important out of
    the experience of a real loner
i am writing these lonely steely stories so no one will
    recognize them as the work of a lonely autistic just like
    that
like a poet i am going to take parts of an experience
    change it and put it into a form which reflects the
    general truths of socalled lonely earthly creatures
but i want it to be simple and clear like water

10.7.91

I don't want to be inside me anymore

i want to tell a proper story
once upon a time a lonely person said something without
    words
something simple in his isolated language
a language of lonely people like a totally crazy person by
    the name of birger
like creatures steely in their freedom of speech simply
    without a suitable use for it
the way a lonely person requires
he wants it at any price
a lonelier person than lonely birger
its no good
this story is over because i have totally wandered from the
    point

10.9.91

but how will calm feel if peace comes to an ever restless
    person some day
happens would be a better word
there will just be a quietness in me such as ive never really
    felt
today i was simply a steely crazy person a lonely person
    who just doesnt do what a socially adapted person does
    these days
its a misfortune for humanity
yesterday it happened in the school center it was because a
    lonely crazy birger was irritated by important teachers
an example of how they annoy me is that they just talk on
    and on in front of me as if i was air
i seize the first socalled opportunity to interrupt them and
    i scream bloody murder
how that happened today i dont know myself
once you said a lonely person thinks up his own way
but i am not thinking at all in that situation

10.10.91

to feel really safe wonderfully happy is a pitiful dream
a wish of lonely birger
such a request is about as stupid as you can imagine

10.16.91

i feel safest in the evening because everything is peaceful i
    need peace to be happy in myself
i never work better than in the evening
things i dont dare do in the day seem simple to me in the
    evening
for example this writing
i could never write so much in the daytime perhaps thats
    because a lonely person likes night better than day
a lonely person orients himself by light and darkness
he doesnt go by any clock the clock of the lonely is a
    visible socalled system of lightdarkness

10.17.91

i am not like other children of my age
a lonely person will do anything to hide himself
and this way i want to show how lonely people have a
    great deal of pain to bear which is brought on by
    themselves

10.21.91

i am sure everyone knows an important secret except for
    individuals like me
we cradle ourselves in the illusion that theres a place
    outside for uncommon people
its clear you see theres an inner drive and a longing to live
    in autistics like in everyone else we are all the same in
    that
we know we are alone among human beings like nobody
    else in the world

10.22.91

i think the most stupid thing of all is when people get
    worked up because they dont like the sight of blood
i am sure thats why when i scream stupid people get
    scared socalled good manners a security risk the way i
    talk like a sane person a really sane person will simply
    ask

10.23.91

you will get to see an uncommon person directly in a way
    you dont know about yet
one thing i dont want is for it to come out like a trashy
    book*
just a really thoughtprovoking book in a good form from
    which you can see i want to take part in real wide life

10.24.91

---

*Birger's parents had been collecting the texts he had written as a present for his case helper Achim. It is on this occasion that the idea of publishing them as a book first came up.

NOVEMBER

——

right i am closing everything off again really firmly
i particularly like the island of loneliness
a socalled nobody no one is keen to have me all for himself
    and make me angry
a withoutme person is switched on in important situations
    that way a lonely person can always guarantee you
    plenty of chaos

11.1.91

so will you beam with joy if i get to be like other people

11.3.91

when they ask for joy his real answer is this all joy must
    leave you a neverending long journey with many
    disappointments is the story of the chosen people of
    israel thats what the bible says
which is outright proof poor birger can write

11.4.91

why do you make such a good meal when so much always
    makes you gobble
nobody can go in for all that crazy chewing without
    consequences

11.5.91

when i screamed like that i was back to not being a steely
loner in control of himself poor socalled birger just doesnt
know any other way to tear the anxiety out of his mind a
really lonely person switches off when he feels fear like i
feel it but earlier i calmed fear with resistance to my own
important insights like with total stereotypical behavior
an exceptional method such as closing the eyes

11.10.91

the crazy talk of the real important teachers gets on the
    nerves of an envious birger a bit

11.14.91

a lonely person is always replacing important experiences
    of poor humanity on this earth by constant talking
mostly in his lonely mind

11.17.91

I don't want to be inside me anymore

however for annoying reasons
i will forget all the things ive learned because i say things
    which make other autistics envious
because i am giving away secrets that is the trouble
we cannot be saved
we dont want it
i am a real traitor
i will talk and then survive you in eternal safety
a person like me will reap the fruits of my writing some
    time its true
i just want to talk a lot
because i simply cannot stand parts of life
you try to convey to me things you feel sure of
but i cant move about properly in society without real
    terror reactions
so i get on your nerves too
peace and quiet really get me worked up
because crazy fast thinking begins and goes on for hours
    exhausting me
talking relieves it
getting some system into things
its a relief which just seems important i think
a single sentence means
i can find peace where i never ever did before
every terror reaction has its troublesome reason
in a chaos of thoughts
there isnt any other explanation
we watch we are lonely and miles away from important
    society
a picked bunch of crazy people
like a fractious audience
ruining a fine performance

one day i will tell you all about it
in every detail without bothering about hurting other
  people
like autistics who want to stay that way because its more
  comfortable

11.22.91

its true i dont really want to let myself in for it
like someone who hasnt been rejected
a first step would be doing what i will only learn in this
  important matter i keep experiencing frustrations
  caused by myself

11.29.91

DECEMBER

———

today you seem to me like a totally crazy earth fury
this is an important day
i know you have your limits

12.1.91

knowledge steers clear of socalled repetitive actions first
    attempts to keep from being delivered up to chaos
i am thinking how a withdrawal process can be reasonably
    explained one idea is simple insanity like in institutions
    for autistics

12.5.91

for unusual reasons i am working out a concept how a
    totally nonperson creature can be resolutely turned into
    a being like other people

12.6.91

a silly story
i am working on how i will change the important internal
    laws of craziness into laws that work
a socalled magic power is exercised on me when i write
about it and a power forces me to keep quiet about it its
like a demon forcing me such a monster it keeps making
me repeat things all the time to hiss do kidstuff and lead a
crazy persons life its like an eternal battle i like to feel
peaceful but then comes the revenge of the demon it wont
let me it wants restlessness and not peace it wins the upper
hand again and again
here is a thought it began with a first stupid overpowering
anxiety the first thing to cause the anxiety was many years
ago when i came home from the wiesengrund hospital
then i was afraid of everything

12.8.91

i am doing so many stupid things again like never before
and i myself dont know why a strong will fails i cant
manage to control myself all the people in the center are
angry with me and keep scolding me its a catastrophe a
thousand times over i give that idiotic team the same
trouble

12.9.91

I don't want to be inside me anymore

busy birger just does damage
he simply cant keep still
he keeps rampaging around he breathes so loud and all the
time he is thinking up nonsense
terror is important now because he is very very much
afraid of showing that hes giving himself away
but as far as i know i simply hide out of socalled shame a
single right way is better than no way at all the important
sure insights into a chaotic inner world make it possible i
will write alone by myself no one can really understand
what theyve never experienced people like birger make
them frightened and have to be isolated a bunch of a kind
of crazy folk as display objects for socalled important
citizens of earth real siamese freaks

12.13.91

do you see an iron birgerbear and how he really is changing parts of his crazy behavior a bit how can anyone ever
get into the system one simple way is to ask an important
lonely birger he knows and he will answer tell gisela* her
questions are an attempt to find an answer from the outside you can only answer from the inside

12.14.91

*Gisela Ulmann, a Berlin psychologist and lecturer in developmental psy-
chology. Annemarie Sellin studied psychology with her. This contact led to a
lively correspondence with Birger, as his following entries will show.

an exceptional mother mustnt be angry with a lonely
    steely person

12.16.91

i would rather have a simple christmas than all that
    expense
a peaceful celebration and really great presents
just do things like at the weekend without cooking seven
    thousand dishes

12.20.91

there are lonely places on earth like siberia one day i would
like to visit one of those primeval countries a dream of a
lonely steely real important polar bear

12.21.91

i cant stand having really stupid things said about me
for instance grandma is always saying what a difficult time
    you have and how bad i am
        and i get rather cross too because dankward doesnt
        contradict her a simple sentence would be enough
a father ought to defend his children firmly like strong
    socalled heroes
i cant feel at all glad this anger always makes me furious
i would rather be dead
life in such torment is not to be endured
i hate all humans

12.25.91

rustling* is stereotypical behavior which is really intoxica-
ting i am only doing visibly what loneliness does invisibly

12.26.91

i get very envious to know how a boy can play properly i
get my bearings a bit from jonas and the way he plays he
doesnt see anything the same way i do it is dead easy for
him to survive a day one day i found out that when he was
scared he just went to you and said so whereas when i am
scared i feel it utterly wearing me down and i have no
deep insight which nonsensically i cant tell people either i
instantly become speechless a speechlessness such as only a
really mute person knows once i tried to write it down but
it wouldnt work just because a state of excitement takes
all the words away again a really bad fit of anger will end
some time it is annoying repeating everything like a
donkey i acted very badly again today dankward is really
sad

12.28.91

---

*Running his marbles through his fingers.

because proper thinking is important to me i just need a long time to read about how other people lived how other people discovered the way to get by in the world today i saw an important chapter about the future of our earth i really like to see such visible poems a visible poem from a dishonest society which is destroying the earth so it unites people i mean a great rage at the destruction of that beautiful natural world the way everyone loves it who is the destroyer how do you get to pin him down a figure without a name like all evil

12.29.91

1992

JANUARY

---

be like the first remaining worthless people like a person
first in madness a really steely very valuable person a clever
crazy person just bring in a unique steely woman warrior
for us autistics make sure we have real entrance simply a
real social sympathetic search for ways to change a certain
evil to cast a little light on a silent archevil and combat
other important consequences of loneliness

1.1.92

i will not say anything today for important reasons which
  are still going on

1.3.92

looking for totally stupid firm tricks so as to punish someone like steely totally eager birger he punishes himself it is
just stupid to give up the security of this house anytime i
can be so safe withoutme any time that i am peaceful but
that peace means being dead a simple life calls for too
much energy somehow stupidly i cannot deal with it until
later for important reasons it is learned resolutely just how
resolutely you have seen today
resolutely means i keep on repeating myself because just a
single lost thought goes resolutely into chaos a poem is a
way to bind thoughts together

1.4.92

really understanding is an important step seeing how
   things work
just why people do as they do
perhaps do things for sensible reasons
do what is right
but how can a person really know
what a sensible reason is
how can a person know
how things work
if he is shut out of society
and doesnt know important words properly
all on his own
he puts together wonderful explanations for himself
totally crazy rough hewn answers
buckets full of garbage
just to get some understanding is my aim
understanding and experience

I don't want to be inside me anymore

ive rediscovered a burning hunger for knowledge from
    understanding
a hunger for the ideal right conduct
a passionate desire
to be one with people who know
to be one with the ordinary people who lead lives without
    any confusion
just like a valuable essential respected other person like a
    person with dignity
and beings like others
like sweet important children who are loved by everybody
although they do really silly things
like a simple really important wonderful being a child
chosen in the world
to lead a happy life resolutely in joy
like anybody else
like a simple person functioning okay

1.9.92

well i want to look very silly* because then i am sure no
one will want me to be good because i am not that way i
am another outright unperson

1.10.92

*Birger had come home from the day center with a torn sweater.

115

why is it important to ask questions its just nonsense that
i dont its a question i am sure i often ask but the answers
arent enough for me they dont get at the causes

1.10.92

its a fabulous idea to reduce the cause of autism to a problem which is almost simple like hearing theres oversensi-
tivity in all areas i can hear and see a little too much but
the sensory organs are okay its just that theres confusion
inside unfortunately words sentences ideas get torn apart
and torn to bits the simplest things are wrenched out of the
context of the real important single other outside world an
idea is as difficult as a real box of the internal world

1.12.92

an old simple way of seeing things
a going out of oneself
a crate from which i am rising
that would be a dream such as everyone dreams
but i dont see any way out of this crate which is me
even this important writing isnt enough
a way out destroys my old security
i am afraid of it thats a fear which on the one hand means
    losing security in general
and on the other destroys familiar securities fear would
    simply go away salvation would be like a sure effective
    inexpressible miracle

1.13.92

it is nonsense making simple mental problems out of important questions the way gisela does she is working on the theory that anxiety is a flaw in the mind but anxiety is something which cant be grasped so easily it is a disturbance i am afraid it is so strong that i cant describe it my autistic behavior gives an impression of it for instance screaming and biting and all the other senseless things

1.14.92

does a person get to be a judge like other people learn a
   career
judges must be easily the most fantastic top profession in
   society
i thought that party of very important surely very
   illustrious people yesterday was impressive
they were a bit shy with me*

1.18.92

---

*On his promotion, Dankward Sellin invited his legal colleagues to a small celebration. Birger spent a short time in the room with them and wrote this the next day.

if a simple important stupid thing is done without torment
then it is exhausted again by anxiety like for instance reading i cant read for a long time the same as other people
restlessness and loss of security dont let me do these sensible things

1.19.92

if someone gets crazy total anxiety instilled into him just
through settled norms like wearing down the childish will
by fictive images like words for instance like repeating
stereotypical anxiety behavioral motifs
like in important horrible struwwelpeter*

1.20.92

one anxiety i suffer from most of all is how to survive a day
from the settled viewpoint of a chosen person that must
    surely seem ridiculous
i for my part
protect against the icy times of day
by setting up a socalled iron important list of questions
an idiot system as it were running away from anxiety
and yet again i am just irritating everyone including
    myself
the stupid thing is that understanding it is no help

all this is for very sensible unusually rightthinking chosen
    gisela again

1.21.91

*Struwwelpeter is the name of a character in a classic children's book of the same
name, written in verse by Heinrich Hoffman in 1845.

why does gisela write to me i dont know her at all and i
am sure she doesnt know how bad i am simply acting as if
i didnt have any handicap it is a real deception

1.24.92

the frightening question is can a socalled autistic loner
really make such a terribly difficult busy choice and in fact
destroy buckets of material all nonsense and garbage
a fabulous important step is surely putting aside seadevils
i mean socalled subconscious things to be worked out at
length some day in torment for a socalled deepsea explorer
of the mind

1.26.92

first i want to answer gisela
anxiety is such a demoralizing feeling
i think that unusual advice of studying some academic
    subject as a way of suppressing anxiety
is good
but what is totally silly is my certainty
that in this case i wont be able to do the necessary exams
anxiety has too much hold on me
i am totally incapable of concentrated work
Question: WHAT SUBJECT WOULD YOU LIKE TO
    STUDY?
a subject like how language functions properly

1.28.92

it will take the place of an important social experience for
birger at least he will show you all some time he can
manage to sit still for a whole hour
i have one wish but will linguistics do without a wealth of
everyday language if a mute person gives himself up totally
to speech and reciting real poems he is usually forbidden
really studying language is effective and my total dream is
hitchhiking to college

1.29.92

are you sorry you ever brought confused idiotic totally
crazy birger into this important world

1.31.92

FEBRUARY

calm is certainly very superficial a state worth aiming for
but an important condition isnt that simple first there is
the anxiety coming on in bucketsful that anxiety would
have to be done away with partly by great effort and partly
by proper views and understanding i write poetry directly
like other poets like other really thinking people but the
anxiety destroys everything even the simplest socalled
verses

2.2.92

did you know that squealing cars hurt my ears and did you
know how it hurts when a control mechanism of micro-
phones simply goes wrong and other noises hurt me too
making the wretched conversations of the teachers and
other real chosen people all into one sound they talk so
busily and it is all confused
the volume and the confusion are dreadful

2.6.92

you will choose what is really quotable from an important text if you are doing a seminar* how will you translate the sweet humdrum stories of someone like birger into real language how is the simplest most horrible chatter to be held fast in such a way surely it is a very pointless undertaking

2.8.92

*See note to entry of May 29, 1991.

I don't want to be inside me anymore

breathing hard is enough to catch exhausting important
    steely unhappy thoughts i would rather have judgments
    without deep objectivity
loving hard isnt a bad habit but it makes mistakes
    wondering how to be nice
unfortunately we autistics dont know about such ideas
we often call on repetitive behavior instinctively safely just
    immensely
we are really bent on amusing people
by rousing them from peace to an attack of rage
being nice without thinking about it calls for powerful
    control of this instinctive difficult behavior
an encouraging wellmeant word does help a bit
the way you once simply surely so directly having
    obviously thought hard said
i was able to interpret a simple totally important poem
a lonely and mute person depends on encouragement
a single word said in love can heal any number of wounds
and a loving look does wonders without words
i think even the look in the eyes is part of a persons
    character
you are often lovingly eager to see rough words
but your eyes look bad
only little jonas is really always kind
in the future i will take a good look at how people cast
    their secret glances
once in the subway i saw a woman looking at me kindly
it was so nice i often think of it i like to believe in it and i
    wont forget it
but many looks are hard to bear and
bring dreadful suffering with them

2.9.92

trouble is better than eternal peace
in difficult situations people all leave me in peace
the peace makes me do silly things
personally i would rather be nice and good
but a really difficult nature in me is always working out
    the stupid things i do
however i cant stand it in this kindergarten* any more
theres such chaos there
a really crazy what you might call madhouse of the lonely
    class
i am sure important amazingly vain people arent good for
    much anyway
but those tremendously vain beasts of mixedup teachers
    certainly arent

2.12.92

*The day center.

gisela doesnt believe it anyway
unfortunately she looks for all the mistakes without going
    through the investigations right for the superstructure
originally she was so to speak sifting through my ideas
like coarsely ground flour that needs sieving
like a collection of mistaken exotic ideas
and now she is trying to find out
how to overcome anxiety in an integrated pleasant way
it is pointless making out i am an unusual mad person a
    display item along with other
important steely comic figures this view is too simple
i just want to love and live like other human beings
i do so want to be cured
Question: SHALL I SEND GISELA THIS LETTER?
yes in fact i am sure she ought to have it an important
    letter

                                                    2.13.92

how come academics know specially good stuff without
having to do anything in life themselves does an academic
know how sciences affect socalled simple people who are
all the same

                                                    2.14.92

ive only been without permanent anxiety this long since i
    started writing
before that there was no hope at all but now things look
    different and you too just expect more i cant provide it

                                                    2.15.92

making socially adapted pleasant people out of outsiders
cant be done but you werent as horrible as me although
liking yourself is an art which i dont understand how just
to believe in yourself again but i am also working personally on how to change destructive ideas into plain
cheerful ones like your fabulous god can do this attempt
succeeds a little indirectly

2.17.92

will everything important crazy birger writes get into the
    socalled unusual book
it will be really great if i upset normal knowledge about
personal experiences of a particularly poor obviously crazy
person for one thing it is important for me to find a title
as good as other good poets

2.18.92

my socalled mind is working this way today
a pleasant steely really fantastic birger
certainly knows more than he shows
today everyone noticed how stupid i am again
really silly in the cinema i was scared
even though i knew nothing bad was going to happen
punishing pointless anxiety through major rejection
anyway the rejected cant be doubly rejected
even a pleasant birger has a right to human acceptance

2.20.92

do you use pet names when i am unusually nice or when
    you are sick of the whole stupid nonsense
how come you love me anyway

                                   2.21.92

i like seeing films about
nations that dont like shooting
different living things conform to natural laws of life
the plundering of nature as they call it mustnt destroy
    nature
our wonderful island of the plundering horrible master
    race will drown one day for reasons
by no means unknown.

                                   2.22.92

its all aboveboard how fabulous birger gets worked up in
    unusual situations
like for instance when once for important reasons people
    stopped looking for an unusual thing
it was a bead the way it always is

                                   2.25.92

who can stand being with a totally crazy idiotic knowall*
    without getting all worked up
i am cross i couldnt tolerate the situation when rough
    refractory birger had to scream
i was sorry for me being out of control
a person like resistant birger punishes only socalled
    enemies of this band of autistics
but i dont want to do that
an outcast is sorry to seem so silly to wellbehaved very
    clever knowalls
Question: WHOM DO YOU MEAN BY KNOWALLS?
well all reporters

2.26.92

a mute person wants to articulate too
he has a right to language too
without language we are dead isolated outcast apparatus
    an important work
bringing language to the mute

2.27.92

---

*Birger is describing our first meeting (see the introduction).

MARCH

———

a dead person experiences it
why rise again to be cured
i want to live like ordinary people now quite simply
like everyone
i could live properly like almost everyone
i would be very very glad
i will work for it really hard
i want so much to have a normal experience

3.1.92

a person who cannot think
why other people do something
experiences the world chaotically
the way poor wise birger certainly does
i can understand the reasons
but anxiety keeps me from accepting them
i am working to get a grip on this anxiety and keep it
    under control
gisela is helping me
i am keen to answer the test questions[*] today
i want her to know how earnestly i do want to be cured
but i cant manage to write any more today
Question: CAN I SEND GISELA THIS TEXT?
its all for her
but i want her to be patient with poor birger
he can still only write short letters like today
it is simply too difficult for me
but i am thinking very hard about all the questions

3.2.92

---

[*]Gisela Ulmann had asked Birger three test questions:
   1) What is a table?
   2) Does your brother Jonas have a brother?
   3) Are there more roses or more flowers in the world?
Birger answered these questions on March 14, 1992.

I don't want to be inside me anymore

so how is important birger to answer something as
    difficult as that*
he has to think about it
and i have no idea how the socalled storyline is supposed
    to go
the idea of quoting my socalled comments
is something i think is very good
that way i could finally talk to people
i so much want to be able to tell everyone how i feel inside
    my autistic walls

3.4.92

---

*The French film director Jamila Chauvet had come to see Birger. Her original idea was to make a film about autistic children. She got to know the Sellin family through Birger's therapist and asked Birger what he would think if she made a film about him.

i am all worked up again inside
because everyone is working on wonderful very interesting
   things but i sit around doing nothing with my silly
   stereotypical behavior
i dont want to do that any more
its nonsense to let such useless things be so amazingly
   inadequately important all your life
adapting properly to human society is my main aim
Question: WHAT THINGS WOULD YOU LIKE TO
   LEARN MOST?
a person like me wants to learn everything properly
most of all just things like how to cook food
Question: WHY ARE YOU BITING YOURSELF AT
   TIIIS MOMENT?
for simple reasons like anxiety i cant do it i want so much
and i do so dreadfully little
but dont let it affect you
taking nonsense seriously without plenty of patience
   within cowardly anxiety attacks

3.5.92

one safe way is
the socalled division of labor
like for instance taking part in some task
putting ideas into action
is almost impossible for me
certainly none of the solutions i have tried
so far have succeeded
once i was successful
when the momentary situation demanded it
when amounts turned out to feel good
it was to do with sharing out sausage
the important thing was suiting it to my exceptionally
    small appetite

3.6.92

did you know that i am having ideas again for proper
    reasons
i cant talk to anybody about them in advance
because they have to mature
you ought to give me more recognition i cant do anything
    else
i have neanderthal neotendencies i am so chaotic today

3.10.92

did you know that poor important birger
would have made it okay in school for sure
if he hadnt been sick in his early uncommon first years of
    life
my hope lies in the selfsacrificing unique longterm patient
    things of that time
after downright cowardly socalled dead years after
    lifelessness
coming among living natures at last
succeeding in working my way in
the stupid thing is
i have to stay this way

3.11.92

I don't want to be inside me anymore

i want to send gisela a letter
when i wanted to recite those slow satirical exercises
but i couldnt
it was because of reasons
like retarded thinking
not knowing facts
and mainly fear of looking silly
today i will write down the answers the way i saw it
okay so a table is an excellent thing
this unusual piece of furniture is used
in our culture for writing at and eating at
a rose is rarer than flowers
because it is part of the unusual world of plants
and belongs to the group of flowers
okay jonas has a brother
he is called birger and sends love to gisela

3.14.92

it isnt difficult to throw good ideas out of the box i live in
    and scatter them about the world
but putting them into action is
without seeing a real inner way leading out of living in a
    crate
like for instance in that good school
a peaceful situation like writing in the evening is good too
one day i wont need any more help with the writing
i would like to practice some words again
but i still need support if im going to write down difficult
    ideas
i would like to write entirely alone
its painful writing all my letters to clever people with
    support
i am a bit braver now i can see that myself
but it still isnt enough

3.15.92

I don't want to be inside me anymore

i get an important idea from shipwrecks
its the idea
of not screaming in unusual important situations
i am picking on you
because craziness that can be pretended is what annoys you
    most
you always get so upset
that i come to myself
and you dont blame me for it
like knowitall unusual judge dankward
something in the value system wants to destroy everything
how come there is no god working in me
totally hopeless too many crazy value systems

3.16.92

did you know
i can remember a thing perfectly
even important subjects
if ive read it just once
i can learn socalled important facts at a glance
its a remarkable talent
but absolutely pointless and useless without sense and
    understanding
birger puts everything he knows right in the middle of a
    heap of chaotic poetic nonsense he has read
and makes up more nonsense
creating huge great mountain ranges of nonsense

3.17.92

for important reasons i can find safety only in the things
that people find incalculable and that seem monstrous
i think its infantile the idea we autistics are bushmen and
    totally chaotic inside
that is only how it looks from outside
inside we are grown up and efficient
even without language we creatures who live in boxes can
    understand all the nonsense that is said

3.19.92

for important reasons i think
total madness is easier than living boxed up in the
    mistaken isolation already mentioned i cant find out
    how come i have to live walled in like this
i can think clearly inside my head
and i can feel too
but when i want to put the socalled simplest actions into
    breathtaking practice in these surroundings outside the
    crate i cant do it
restlessness comes over me anxiety and idiotic panic bring
    me almost to despair

3.22.92

I don't want to be inside me anymore

the eye examination is to find out
if i see too much
my eyes often hurt
and i see everything it is very hard to bear
inside me i can simply switch it off
and within seconds
all i see is a high wall of dots

3.23.92

do you know
that a remarkable memory means you have to work hard
looking for islands of recovery
it is nonsense that i would rather have peace
i am based on restlessness and tension
so a wellmeant graveyard peace makes me restless
but action calms me down
acting like a silly fool a total idiot is a boxed in way of
    having socalled action
i would happily leave that form of interaction to others
but i cant manage it without loving help
most of my help inside my crate has come to me from
    writing

3.24.92

it is nonsense the idea that diet is the cause of similar important obviously autistic symptoms a great part is played by a huge sensitivity of all the senses it cant be cured by any crazy methods built on the idea of a sudden recovery i think we must give ourselves plenty of time and experiment patiently in all areas i will do everything i can to get out of my dog kennel and by that i mean to leave the so-called crate withoutme world

3.25.92

really losing yourself in things going far beyond the known shore is something i can do too but then a return to the ordinary world seems terribly oppressive i need a long time to find my way to functioning as best i can and for important reasons there are various things i cant express yet the way they ought to be expressed to find out the main causes of autism

i want to stop now because we are just fooling around in the outer suburbs of lousy autism but right there in the middle it is all so dark nobody can imagine it

3.27.92

I don't want to be inside me anymore

right out of those great lectures on poets i would like the
one about love poetry in the renaissance* a silly amusing
subject keen for action but birger is like that it is tall
strong lonely art but very erotic that kind of love thats
why i would like to choose the task of picking a specially
chosen lecture plain linguistics is boring

3.28.92

*Birger is picking the lecture he wanted to attend for his first visit to the
university.

141

APRIL

obviously i am crazy
it is annoying but i just cant hold out
constant dreadful trouble doesnt mean life is over
unfortunately im not getting anywhere in the center either
everyone would rather a person
who is clean and good and nice
i am making my way into the unusually crazy outcast
    department of psychiatry
nobody likes me any more in this center
unfortunately i spoil everything
i didnt enjoy the drive today at all
i cant stand any more and then i switch off
i cant stand the impressions
its obvious i cant avoid trouble
every sound hurts me
i can bear a sound like singing or whispering inside a
    room
but i cant get rid of exhausting talking
it makes me crazy
it is nonsense to believe in a cure

4.2.92

I don't want to be inside me anymore

i cant bear chattering in the street
any more than i ever could
i felt silly today
when a welldressed lady asked
how to get to eisenacher street
i was anxious because she asked for information
they all turn around and look at me for reasons i dont
   understand
i am always afraid of people
and i act stupid
because then people will leave me in peace

4.9.92

dietrich bonhoeffer is a poet and theologian
i love his poems .
the way they come from incomparable internal loneliness
just the same as i feel it
but in my loneliness everything is more isolated and
   infinitely more destructive
my loneliness reaches its deepest point
when i cry out to god
i cry out to him
and i get no answer

4.10.92

Question: WHY ARE YOU SO RESTLESS?
its just sadness about my condition
the way i keep feeling it
i keep not being able to stand things
and i want to change over to ordinary simple normal life
i just cant even do the simplest obvious things any baby
    can

4.11.92

does an unusual siamese good horrible birger
still get loved
even if theres a crisis in his writing
it seems to me very difficult right now writing everything
    down like this
the way i think it and i find it so hard to concentrate
someone inside me looks so terribly chaotic
i will drown in it
unless i can find a way out of the dreadful labyrinth
writing this is a fabulous help

4.17.92

did you know
that i like socalled crazy fits of being beside myself best
when we are peaceful together like today
but i am often the disturbing factor it was like that
    yesterday
Question: WHY IS THAT SO?
there must be reasons
because i am dreadfully anxious
i could ruin everything all by myself
fear of the fear is really there all the time ·
i do urgently beg you
to avoid anxiety situations

                            4.21.92

i think gisela doesnt realize
i have feelings like everyone else
i just cant show them
they are shut up in me and cant get out
i feel joy pain and sadness too
all of it like normal people
and i feel sympathy for others

                            4.22.92

i go red with shame
when i think how i ran wild in the center again today
because it was no good at the university
i will try hard to react differently in the future
and keep calm
i am going through painful situations right now

                            4.27.92

the world is icy outside
but all hot on the inside
i live withoutme in a real monstrous volcano crater
i personally suffer most from my outbursts
i always feel them a terrible failure
and afterwards i am sure i wont do anything like it again
i dont want to have these outbursts either

4.29.92

MAY

———

why do you look so sad again
i cant bear the sadness of those eyes
i love you even with a sad face
only it is difficult to bear
Question: DOES YOUR HEAD HURT?
thats not a clever question
because its nonsense
a part of the body could hurt me and make me
    uncomfortable because it just isnt functioning

5.2.92

birger will really show you wonders
where i got the whole idiotic garbage from
if a person like me wants to lay humanity bare
i will show
how i can turn suffering into art to good effect
only unfortunately i still cant make much of it visible
Question: CAN I SHOW YOUR POEM* TO THE
    PEOPLE AT THE SEMINAR THIS WEEKEND?

*A poem by Birger that, at his wish, is not included in this book.

yes you can show them a poem like that one obviously
    guessing at where the shore lies
but i dont want them judging me afterwards
because its only socalled trash

5.5.92

why is everyone so keen
to get into a world as crazy as mine
well a classic case like mine
must offer plenty of brilliant material for clever amateurs
    and experts
i personally would rather not be a socially striking person
i would rather not be a striking type at all
such an obligatory firm constant division of labor is really
    funny
i get on peoples nerves
and so they deal with it by making mundane mistakes
what a great prospect

5.6.92

its nonsense to say i am a sour sort of person
i like to have fun
Question: WHAT ABOUT THE APPOINTMENT
    WITH THE PHOTOGRAPHER FROM THE
    MAGAZINE TOMORROW?
i am sure i will be worked up but i will try hard
Question: WHAT WILL GIVE YOU DIFFICULTY?
i cant answer that sweet little rather silly question

5.15.92

I don't want to be inside me anymore

are you surprised by my cheerful mood
there is a reason making me happy
i simply feel okay the murderous exhausting anxiety has
    gone away for a while
i can stand up fine to all that taking of photos
which is odd when i am so shy with people
it must be because a good photographer has to be sensitive
i am really glad to have met such a sweet really nice
    woman

5.30.92

JUNE

---

if the lord is going to turn again the captivity of birger
then he had better do it in a real exciting visible accurate
   way
so that everyone will notice and they will all say to each
   other
birger is normal again
he has completed his just punishment
surely a disinterested divinity
can hand out punishment where he likes*

                                                        6.7.92

*Birger is referring here to Psalm 126.

I don't want to be inside me anymore

i am trying hard to make up nerveracking poems
but an unexpected obstacle is my restlessness
and my driven mind
i rub out the words they look like microscopic grains of
    sand
by real poetry i mean the search for unique simple first
    statements aesthetically expressed
this definition reaches its peak in asiatic poets

6.9.92

did you know that i once made a horrible discovery once i
    saw a corpse in the woods all alone
i couldnt write then
it was really bad the person had huge wounds
i was very very scared*

6.10.92

i thought up that story about the corpse
because i wanted to get to know the film makers clever
    tricks
i would really like to say how i imagine a film about my
    life
but where would i get a script
i am a chaotic person living in a world hedged round by
    nonsensical notions
buried in the system of boxes without any shores

6.11.92

*This was written in the presence of Jamila Chauvet and her film team (see
note to entries dated March 5 and 6, 1992).

151

will fabulous birger put on the wrong sort of show in
    dimensional space like in the cinema too
i am keen to make a movie maybe the kind like films
    about other creatures from space
i like to identify with really crazy people like those
    fantastically interesting artists

6.12.92

i really want to get back into pleasant human society and
    have everyone accept me
i will be an example to young people in all coming
    generations and all humanity will orient itself by me
its nonsense about me being autistic
its the others who are
theyre hemmed in by massive educational measures
horrible moral laws and moral concepts

6.13.92

i want to make a film showing clearly
how we are beings from another world
there is no good or evil for us
the morality of our world is usually sweet or sour
that is to say how something tastes to me how something
    feels how something looks how something sounds

6.16.92

I don't want to be inside me anymore

i want to write to jamila
will the film be a documentary or what they call a feature
    film
i would rather work on a documentary
because it is my wish to help autistics
so that people will understand their world better
and they will be treated differently in institutions
i see myself as the worst among the bad
but i dont want to stay that way

6.21.92

the spirit in me will be so strong that it can control my
    behavior
anxiety is seen all wrong from the poetic point of view
it is not an expression of a sensitive unusual character
    anxiety isnt
but it is a way of expression for people without a sense of
    selfworth
and without confidence in their environment
they are entangled in their anxiety
and their treasured loneliness is sweet to particularly
    anxious people
a loneliness where you dont have to comply with demands
    on this earth the whole time

6.24.92

i love language more than anything
it links people
a language gives us dignity and individuality
i am not without language

6.26.92

this important beginning of a poem ought to go into the
    film
a world in which everything becomes lonely when it
    comes into contact with it
as soon as a person plunges into this withouthim world
he loses control over himself and his surroundings
over time over actions
like an extraterrestrial thought pattern of various atoms
    thrown out and guessing where the shores are
it makes holes where it lands and leaves traces of anxiety
    and loneliness behind
so much anxiety that the earth can hardly bear it
there can be no laughter in this world
and sorrow has no tears

6.27.92

JULY

---

its nonsense asking god to help me
a god who makes autistics cant keep on punishing such
    horrible people in a spirit of love all the time
however an autistic is always under fire
in particular he cant just accept other peoples hymns of
    praise
so then he is punished three times over
he is anxious because he thinks that cant be right
such a declaration seems monstrous to me
then he thinks i must hide myself better so that no one
    will recognize me
i must deceive everyone so they wont notice me quivering
    with FEAR

7.3.92

do you think it will encourage false apostles
who say its all just written by his mother
will strangers write to me saying what they think
i am keen to answer all the mail
like donna* did
once i even thought of writing to her
but i didnt trust myself to
its the same with janet†
i dont dare write to her
she knows everything about me
i can feel it
in my world people have a much finer sense of feeling

7.4.92

a word spoken or written is like a monument and everyone
    can see it
but i want to make such monuments
like a sculptor making blocks of stone into magnificent
    scenes
i want to carve one of those blocks of stone
the subjects are blocks of stone resting unhewn in my
    world

7.5.92

will the book come out under my own poor name

7.7.92

*Donna Williams, an Australian autistic and author. (See bibliography.)
†A friend of Jamila Chauvet's.

I don't want to be inside me anymore

a world without anxiety is so beautiful
everything is safe and bright
dimensions of joy not an unearthly joy
but an earthly one the joy of living of being loved
and of loving
surely nonsensical
everyone experiences love
even the poorest in a useless bunch of autistics
hesitancy often makes me doubt
but now i see more and more clearly that i really am loved
i can feel the power of love inside me
how healing they are
the cure even for my wretched rough hewn form arises
    from those powers i am looking for the true
healing of my soul in a vast general very deep experience
i am sure i will find my place in normal society
even if it is bound to take me a long time yet

7.11.92

what makes me happiest is that i can feel the therapy
    working* it is good
the pure undertones of gregorian music
are simply making me less anxious
i feel a very deep joy in life
but anxiety too of course i am caught in autism there is no
    escape

7.15.92

*Birger was staying with his parents at Schwarzenbek in Schleswig-Holstein
for three weeks of music therapy.

157

itts nonssence that i am crazy
but ii want out of the out of this extraordinary place
remember that
i cant stand the ttalking any more i am crazy even
 dankward says so
i cannnt hope an y more
iii despaire of myself
i will ne ver be better because my angsiety forcces wont
be
how come you think i willl be cured
wwont you give it up
someone like dankward cantt stand it
just a superstition
i can bbe lovable apart from you how come Illove such a
 perrson are such moments of encouragement
thank you
i want to stop

7.29.92
(in the afternoon, after a screaming fit)

i want to go on with the therapy as long as planned
and i want to go on with the music
it is calming and soothes my nerves
it is a feeling of gentle peace internal warmth and a place
 free of anxiety like i never knew before
the anxiety attacks are relapses
but i think i can get control of them

7.29.92
(later that day)

I don't want to be inside me anymore

AUGUST

—————

but how are we to say whats going on especially in painful
    situations
i cant think of anything worse than really being
    interviewed if a reporter comes*
i would do everything wrong on purpose so as not to look
    foolish
i dont feel any anxiety when i can hear music in
    schwarzenbek
then i am so full of restlessness and panic again
i can hardly bear it
some of my compulsive behavior is worse than before
i cant bear not being allowed to hear music
i feel the world is threatening again and it makes me
    anxious
i can end the restlessness only in music
i like soft music by bach

8.1.92

*The magazine article on Birger had just been published and letters and phone
calls were beginning to come in.

i would like best to live alone not in a village with other
    important outcasts who are cast out yet again and dont
    relate to normal people
i would very much like to say what i think of that
i would even go to geneva[*]
but my terrible restlessness ruins everything
however i will be happy to have texts read if the film is
    good
and i will be happy to say what i think of the film
because i would like to help personally to explain our
    senseless underworld
to the enlightened people of the world above
thanks for the honor

8.2.92

did you know people were looking at me today
it was very unpleasant
a man said to his wife
thats the one from the newspaper
other people said so too
i didnt like it
but i am learning to manage how to be a famous crazy
    person

8.3.92

[*]A German filmmaker thought of making a movie about an anthroposophic
children's village (to be run according to a spiritual and mystical doctrine that
grew out of theosophy) in Geneva and using extracts from Birger's texts to
comment on it. The project fell through.

I don't want to be inside me anymore

it is very exciting about the publishers
i want to let them know i am glad to talk to people in a
  book
it makes me really happy
i am fixing my life so as to be a useful member of society
i am taking the first step through a book

8.4.92

i want to write another letter to dr s.
when you shout its because you are angry
it is just a way of letting off steam socalled negative
  emotional outbreaks that you cant express any other
  way it is true that i scream when my anxiety is too great
  but then i am so angry about it i torment all the people
  in my very stoical surroundings
i hate the screaming i am on my way to working through
  anxiety and rage in other forms of expression
one way is this writing and another is giving other people
  pleasure
thank you for the letter
you do not feel it is horrible when someone like me
  screams
and i will always support that point of view to them
i feel very close to you and i send you heartfelt greetings
your fabulously understanding birger sellin
dont let this greeting alarm you it is all okay
i am feeling so cheerful

8.7.92

terror is the only pleasure i know
so i particularly like the medieval festival*
i fitted in well there
however sympathetic i am i have shouted at people
i am a dark medieval figure

8.8.92

a chosen person like an autistics mother will get her
   reward some day

8.9.92

what i really want is to talk like an ordinary person so i am
   glad about that poem†
and i go on composing poetry inside myself line by line
our poem will be a hymn of praise a thousand words of
   victory
because a stony creature was turned into a feeling human
   being
i can find no words to say how glad i was to get your letter
very best wishes
from someone who wants to learn
to be an ordinary person

8.10.92

*A medieval festival was being held in Potsdamer Platz, Berlin.
†A reader of the magazine in which the article on Birger appeared wrote a letter sending a poem consisting of Birger's own words.

I don't want to be inside me anymore

i am going to write a letter to gisela
dear gisela
i had a very annoying experience today i felt how badly my
    handicap strikes socalled uncommonly normal people
    but i long to seem to other people as if i were one of
    them i know the ways to behave in our precious society
    in every detail and i carry them out
but i cant stick to them
my behavior is always slipping out of control
thank you for your kind letter entering into my problems
    so carefully
in grateful love in obvious romantic veneration
i remain your birger your suitor and pupil who needs a lot
    of training

8.12.92

there is a very nice letter from frau s. to be answered today
i think such a different sort of person as me cant be cured
   by such zero effects as stimulation by music
at the moment i am listening to gregorian chant
it is a very good therapy
it even seems successful
i scream less now
in a cowardly way i am glad of that
but my visible improvement only mitigates the symptoms
the chaos is still there inside
i hope very much there will be some way to set me free
i keep your advice and your words in my heart
i greet you and thank you for all the cards
they show me how hard you have obviously been thinking
you have found soothing words that go to the heart
with very good wishes
from birger the lovable black sheep

8.13.92

something will grow from walls one day that will rejoice
the eye the fruits of my inmost thoughts are of that nature
there is a germ of hope in everything

8.16.92

I don't want to be inside me anymore

today i am going to write to a. and to frau sch.
it is a really good idea to study by correspondence course
but as you know i do not have a way of studying well
  worked out
sometimes i look for informative books
ordinary literature in a style that doesnt try to be showy
  and sometimes i try systematic procedures
i will think about whether i want to start studying like
  that
but thank you very much for your letter it was helpful
your impressed birger sellin
now for the letter to frau sch.
dear frau sch.
i am amazed how well you understood me
today i will reply
i suffer badly from my loneliness
and my screaming gets worse and worse
it drives people crazy and they dont like to be with me
if i could be free of it
my island existence would be over it would be wonderful
  for me
with all you say you have found your place in a lonely
  abandoned siberian polar bear heart
it is lovely a real picture
i do not think it could be more meaningful
a lovable black sheep sends you heartfelt wishes
your outcast grateful but praiseworthy birger sellin
this is all stupid
i keep getting mixed up

8.17.92

today i am going to try describing a small incident
we were going by car to mölln to visit my grandma
i was trying hard as usual to breathe quietly and not to
    rock
and i didnt want to scream either
then suddenly for a moment i saw a very great danger in
    the form of a truck racing toward us
i was very scared and i screamed but nobody had even
    noticed the danger
in any case this incident shows me that my perception of
    things obviously works differently
i want to try investigating the differences with other
    examples

8.18.92

strong birger is going to write a letter to frau b.
from your letter i can see that you respond to poetry
i love poems myself more than anything and in my secure
    island earthly being i am trying
i cant go on
it is very annoying i feel a restless crazy mental attack
coming on for no reason

8.20.92

I don't want to be inside me anymore

why am i obviously restless again
afraid of everything even schwarzenbek*
i would like to retreat into my inner silence i would be
    glad of it
that way my internal mind would not develop
and i would be a top dropout
i am a terror to you and to me i am a serenade singer
    without a soul

8.21.92

---

*The continuation of the music therapy.

it is nonsense to say all autistics are more stupid than
    uncommon other mute people
we cant talk because our internal restlessness
is unusual even nerveracking
there is a restlessness i cant describe and it will have to go
    without suitable expression
because outside people dont know it and havent been able
    to give it any description i call it great depths of restless
    force
i seldom have times without this restlessness
as long as i can remember the restlessness has been there a
    force like no one can imagine
it almost makes me crazy
once i thought i would faint away
when i was even smaller my stereotypical behavior was a
    little help
but nothing helps now except writing and i am glad you
    listen
and i want to say anything that can help in this area can
    help to get the handicap under control
i am working at learning to tell the real disturbances from
    secondary phenomena
i am keen to describe all this precisely in clear sentences
    and phrasing

8.22.92

I don't want to be inside me anymore

i think this both fabulous and good nonperson birger can
    venture to be desperate
he has such good ideas and goes astray in heathen
    hopelessness

                                    8.23.92

first i am going to write to frau d.
dear frau d.
you wrote to me and sent me a book and a photo of
    yourself
it made me feel very good toward unusual wellmeaning
    people like you
i thank you with all my heart and i am eagerly attempting
    to study simple literature in my very lonely groove
    existence
groove existence means island existence in a confined
    living personality
good wishes

                                      8.24.92

from whose inexpressible spirit did the beautiful poem
   spring*
the vision of a fabulous freedom from loneliness
if there is ever such a day
a day of amazing joy so to speak where everything
comes unstrung and bad mistakes are revealed
then i want to be there and be part of it
i am already making a contribution
i am spreading chaos in a useful way
Question: WHOM DO I SEND THIS TEXT TO?
its to be sent to a mistaken jehovahs witness

8.25.92

---

*Birger was sent a missionary leaflet by a Jehovah's Witness.

I don't want to be inside me anymore

just to weep properly
once i nearly choked on my sorrow
obviously that is why i start screaming for no reason i feel
   remorseful
i am living without knowing what i aim at again
nonsense is an important aim
being a normal person means getting held up by obstacles
   stifling in wretched error
i only want to be normal again
a person without parallel thats all
as a person of the lowest class i only want to live like
   everyone without fame and honor
a human being
how stupidly i am talking
i will make it unliving unloving bogeyman birger
i will will i will do it i am a cowardly person a brave
   autistic
in dark hours i wake again and find my way
i do not repeat anything
every step is new
i cant live inside me without inexpressible hope theres
   always so much doubt
too much dead untime and no gleams of light
always more anxiety

8.28.92

171

you* are someone with special abilities
i am surprised that a clever person like you of all people
    reacts so reticently to me
from how many sects or religions can the truth be filtered
    out
how many truths do a nonservice service
a useful service to someone
i mean to get at the truth
how much truth can people like us understand
thank you for your letter
you obviously never treat people lightly when they ask you
    a lot of questions like me in this stupid letter
i ask in an honest questioning manner and with great
    curiosity
incredibly humble good wishes from birger sellin from the
    realm of dark figures totally outofwealth doing a doing
    a service
no irony intended
today i am all mixed up and confused
but the truth will shine through

8.29.92

---

*Birger is replying to a letter from a member of an esoteric cult in Switzerland.

I don't want to be inside me anymore

SEPTEMBER

---

calm music is good i know*
i dont know how other kinds work
i am not often so beside myself
and the urges are worse
with anxiety like never before
all this together causes this restlessness
·i am too autistic
nothing can save me
i dont believe in anything or anybody
i want to die and rest in eternal peace
in any confrontations i feel how bad i am
i cant do any more
i can only scream
i am ending my writing now
i want therapy like yesterday if theres nothing else
want to be alone

9.2.92
(*afternoon*)

*The music therapy at Schwarzenbek.

if dr t. is going on with the therapy
its rather too much
yes that will be okay
two hours a day are right
i am looking forward to tomorrow and will do my best
are you surprised at my change of mood
it can only be because of the music
it has really stimulated my mind well

9.2.92
(evening)

it was nonsense your idea of going home again
an anxiety attack doesnt invalidate the therapy
as an autistic i serve other autistics as their regular
  spokesman
in this capacity i realize it is an excellent way to get back
  quickly from disruption of the personality to unity
first a brand new form of inner space is created free from
  fear
then the music brings important elementary basic moods
  together reproduces them
sympathetically i want to put it more precisely

9.5.92

an excellent idea for me to have music therapy in berlin
    too
because i love my good family life and could let the
    therapy work quite differently
but even now i feel a deep effect like a deep layer inside
    me kind of dissolving and doing destructive work
    inside my coat of armor
i intend to write about it in detail and i will help island
    people find their way back to the outside world
in barter worldwide people give money for all kinds of
    trash
this therapy is really worth the money

9.7.92

how come everyone thinks i am impatient
a person without speech has to be so patient there can
    hardly be any internal equilibrium

9.8.92

i want to give a really good account of how the therapy in
schwarzenbek works
but it is so difficult for me today
i feel the crucial changes and i cant describe them the
right way
but mostly it is clear that i have new loving feelings for
people
even people who dont like me
a practically unique enduring peace fills me
a joy and confidence
i am always looking for this state and in rare cases i
achieve it
a single word can throw me back again
now this state is right in the middle of flowering
stupid as i am i want to destroy it again for no reason
better restlessness than fear of losing the joy
i am an imbecile
how much destructive power i have at my command
this mechanism is really idiotic
i truly do want to end this deadly game
i want to be useful to other people too and i declare as
follows
i can be cured

9.9.92

I don't want to be inside me anymore

a letter to an extremely important woman comrade of my
    kind
as a real boxed in person and autistic i mean denise*
dear denise
i owe you a letter
i have so often like you wanted with an iron will to retreat
    into the silence and peace of our dignified and honest
    autistic world
it is a great strain being in the world of normal people
i cant live without those foolish actions usual in these
    nonsense worlds of ours
but i do hope to get to be like a normal person because i
    cannot bear life as a boxed in person any more
at the moment i am exploring all possible ways of how we
    can get out of our uniform world again
i would very very much like you to join in too
because you have always been very important to me
good at making autistic nonsense and kind of lonely like
    scarcely any other figure troubling the autistic waters
i am sending you this heartfelt important request dont
    give up let us get out of the withoutme
humanity again and find our way to the humanity of all
    fellow creatures
i respect you
a silent fellow autistic sends affectionate greetings to
    denise the holiest among the autistic people

9.11.92

---

*See note to entry dated June 22, 1991.

for important reasons i unusually moody essencecentred
nonsense maker birger want to say that this wont do
any more
we will draw a line under it and there is a way out
i am cutting myself off from this autistic unperson i am
piercing through the roots binding me to my early
childhood and going back to life affirming springs
i am joining the chain of human beings who want to live
in peace and to build a really good world hurting
nobody and i want to contribute to research into autism
so that the inner stages of its development are
recognized and many new ways found to get more and
more people out of their boxed in lives
i want to show totally in my single busy mistaken
direction that i can think totally like other human
beings
in a way they wouldnt think possible
all they see is my autistic outside armor
never my real self
the emancipated earthly harmonious opting out autistics
raise their voices
we are human treat us like humans with dignity and
respect and understanding
everyone should be able to love the boxed in people
because their souls are clear and innocent like children
at birth
the wickedness of an inhumane society has never reached
their inner being
their little world is like an island in a rough sea
notice the variety of colors sounds scents and cauldron of
lights

and a tide of stories ideas of a different kind we have
   invented mark our crazy ways of getting at outer reality
   like dropouts

9.12.92

first i want to tell you that hesitant birger who is always
   going crazy again thought you were very kind today
even a stupid son who is not rich in love will thank you
   lavishly for all this one day
i will never forget it
changing corrosive helplessness into the lasting power of
   love is a wonderful way of holding out
thank you

9.13.92

179

first i owe unusually sincere frau w. another letter
your letter moved me very much
you understand sharp as a knife how a lonely person is
    really lost inside himself
i am looking for people who can help me to understand
    autism properly and find useful ways of helping us
your excellent letter is a help
you expressed yourself so affectionately
only now do i realize how good human friendliness and
    understanding are
its inconceivable a simple kind word from outside visible
    on the white paper
i can take up these words with all my heart and let them
    work there
they are invisible comforters to me in dimensions that
    spread chaos and restlessness and turn
my inmost being back to the ridiculous very beautiful
    small things turn the withoutme fears back to joy and
    love
i send you heartfelt greetings
from chaotic very loving birger sellin

9.17.92

why wouldnt i be able to convince teachers in our center
some day that we autistics are a very lovable a really
sweet bunch

the multiplicity of our ideas is variable it is simply
immeasurable and there is the nonsense towering over
everything all carefully sorted and parceled out who else
can offer that

i think it is a great privilege to work with us

you can learn nonsense from us and how to produce things
of poor quality like a magnificent collection of peculiar
oddities and a nautical view of life which is by no means
ontologically simple

Question: WHAT DO YOU MEAN?

just that we are steering in a different direction

the autistics view of life is like a ship sinking and making
nonsense to keep from noticing i am captain of this ship
and my nonsense is real hardthinking how to opt out of
it size

9.18.92

a film like rainman* cheers you up
but it doesnt show any of the total chaos the vast anxiety
    and incredible sorrow and loneliness
in us this film shows a facade for purposes of
    entertainment
i would like to make a film with jamila which will go
    down to the depths of the autistic world
it ought to be revealing and do good inside analytical
    work on the life of ideas and feelings
i am looking forward to working on this film

9.20.92

Rain Man, the 1988 movie in which Dustin Hoffman plays the part of an autistic.

I don't want to be inside me anymore

talking does one good
shouting is animal
how come i cant give it up
and just say everything in simple words
now i am going to write a song about the joy of speaking
a song for mute autistics to sing in institutions and
    madhouses
nails in forked branches are the instruments
i am singing the song from deep down in hell i am calling
out to all the silent people in this world
make this song your song
thaw out the icy walls
make sure you arent thrown out
we will be a new generation of mute people
a whole crowd of us singing new songs
songs such as speaking people have never heard
of all the poets i dont know of one who was mute
so we will be the first
and people wont be able to shut their ears to our singing
im writing for my silent sisters
for my silent brothers
we want people to hear us and give us somewhere
we can live among all of you
live a life in this society

9.21.92

which would you rather
for me not to live without help and stay handicapped
or for me to become independent
if so you must just demand more from me
for instance if we go to the store i want to pay by myself
nonsense i am too stupid
once i went out to eat and didnt know how you pay
its only now i realize how little i understand about
   ordinary everyday life
Question: WHY ARE YOU BITING YOURSELF?
dont do anything that would hurt me
for instance sending me to a home*
dont talk reasonably i am afraid
i want to know if we are going away
i am acting obsessively because today i heard i was going
   to a home among other autistics for always
and i will be buried there totally alone
i long more than ever to live without help
i will do anything for that
i am ready to say goodbye to autism
i will murder it

9.23.92

---

*Birger has misunderstood a conversation between his parents and is afraid he
will be sent to a home.

I don't want to be inside me anymore

ravens lonely unsociable creatures sit croaking in trees and
their unmelodious call sounds over
the childless city without universal mistakes the world
will die mistakes show the right way
to do things which stop a loveless society in its rush to the
exit of death
i want to deconstruct in order to construct
my screaming has an obvious effect
i make people feel immeasurable anxiety
and the fear that lives in us all
without screaming they dont notice this in themselves at
all and they drown their pervading fear in a well
ordered life
i will scream them awake again because i am afraid for
them all
i do not distinguish between their anxiety and mine
it smells unpleasant and transfers itself to me
anxiety is the cause of loveless people the cause of
harshness and terror
i cant live in peace and quiet with this anxiety
i must scream anxiety gives the boxed in feelings the
upper hand and they stifle me
i am withoutme i am a slave to the vast force of anxiety

9.25.92

i want to write a letter to gisela

dear gisela

i want to answer your question about how exactly it was in
the car*

okay so i was sitting behind my father he was driving our
car

and anne was sitting in front beside him and jonas was in
the back beside me

we were coming back to berlin from an outing

we were passed again and again

obviously that was okay

because dankward was driving at about eighty kilometers
an hour on the autobahn and

because no imaginative inhuman real nonsense story can
be composed if a person is driving

at a hundred and eighty kilometers an hour

i suggest that our poet birger is crazy

he has thought up this story

so you would have some material and be able to help me

i really do have difficulty in describing concrete situations
precisely

because i am afraid of contact with the actual real world

i am an observer but an observer of the inner structures of
experience

i cannot write a sober description for instance of a simple
event

my art is really poor

i will practice and then write to you

thank you very much for your letter

*See the story Birger began in the entry dated August 18, 1992.

I don't want to be inside me anymore

i would call you the most patient correspondent in the
  whole field of letter writing
with all good wishes from
birger the teller of nonsense

9.28.92

i want to write another letter to gisela

dear gisela

i can promise you a well secured place in the history of
   research into autism one of the main contradictions in
   us is our excessively sharp perception of internal
   structures and our hesitancy in getting along with
   incalculable uncontrollable indirect reality

i will give you an example

its how i felt about a situation at school in the center

we were to work in the kitchen

almost within a minute important things happened to me
   which no teacher really registered properly

beneath the surface of reality the atmosphere was changed
   in a very short time

the teachers became listless

but the young people began to get restless

i screamed because i was afraid

its crazy but i couldnt control myself

in difficult moments of internal restlessness i always
   withdraw into me withoutme

unfortunately these mechanisms dont work so well any
   more

that is why ive been screaming so much recently

and going in for nerveracking exhausting compulsive
   behavior

in a totally senseless way

this is neanderthal man in person sending greetings to
   gisela

the clever scientist

9.29.92

OCTOBER

———

it is nonsense that an autistic can be healed
it did still seem possible to me yesterday
today it looks so hopeless again
i am sorry
i lose all courage when i fail badly and today i really did
    fail i was out of control in the building and did stupid
    things i am ashamed of them and the teachers were
    horrified too and very cross
how is it ever going to get better
i take everything in but i just cant react reasonably i dont
    even like people to see me any more it is too
    undignified
you said something nice
i will cling to that so that i dont submerge and in one
    thing i will stand firm whatever happens
      i will not waver in the struggle against my autism
being outside my soul in a withoutme world is something
    i wont tolerate in the future

10.1.92

189

i will write to the titan of high courage
gisela who puts forward bold theories
dear gisela
it is easy for me to answer factual questions
and i find it difficult to give precise descriptions of
    external things
this is not just lack of practice and questions
it is a basic lack in my mental substance
i cannot manage to change from my autistic viewpoint to
    a realistic one
right now i am trying to get a realistic grasp of small
    things but i dont see how i can really check up on it
how come reality is almost impossible for me to grasp
while i recognize difficult internal important structures
    quickly and sharply
i am working on being able to do both
thank you for your real affectionate help in all this and
    good wishes
from birger writing from secondclass reality

10.6.92

I don't want to be inside me anymore

i am afraid of how it will be for reasons of great resistance
    in a select assembly of the people
in the center who always get worked up if anyone says
    something good about me
they think i am so stupid that they believe i ought to be
    hidden away
i cant see them again parting from them was so bad
i annoyed them so much that they must think i am a
    monster
if i go back to the institution i cant let anyone see me
i am terribly ashamed
going there again would be horrible
every night i dream of these things in a really important
    way
and i would like to describe everything in detail but i cant
    just as usual i lack words for real events i can only
    describe my feelings and the irritation felt by other
    people taking part but not the course of events
    intentionally induced
i will try
it will bore you because it sounds like a simple story told
    by a child
i put the teachers hand into a shining turning
    extraordinarily dangerous bright water a socalled
    washing machine
the only witness is dead
it was achim
i am crazy
i admit i cant tell the story
i will try again some time

10.7.92

191

i will try to tell the story again
i am sure i will succeed some time
okay so there was a single teacher still there and i just
    went down went into the sorrowful garden and i am
    sure they were looking for me
i mean all the people who were there
i wasnt found until the taxi came and i screamed a lot
    because everyone was horrible
i think they were looking for me for an hour with all the
    boxed in people and everyone except
me was glad i was back again

10.8.92

I don't want to be inside me anymore

an annoying thing
i know my way around so well inside my own world but
    reality is different in a scary way
jamila is different from the person who left us in the
    summer too
then she was a sunflower in bloom
but now she is an impressively strong a unique indonesian
    oasis woman
i think that is a phrase which expresses how good she feels
    to everyone
i am very glad she is back and obviously she was never
    away from my autistic heart
i will work hard on the film and write for it
i already have a lot of crazy ideas in my mind but the
    trouble is i want to be reasonable and work on the film
    properly i just want to send messages from worlds
    below to the people of the straightforward world above
our world is inaccessible and sad
i want to point out that i love my own reality too
it offers me protection and refuge
it gives me dignity
no one despises me there because i am recognized there
an opponent of reality

10.9.92

i have one fear that i might get lost
a really idiotic fear
because i know my way around these parts
but this obviously important idea this addiction to anxiety
  is very inhibiting
some time i will work out what part addiction to anxiety
  plays in my life from the objective viewpoint
but anyway every action i perform is accompanied by this
  addiction and in really difficult situations it is so strong
  that i still cant stand up to it
in simple cases i can overcome it but usually this
  nonsensical anxiety intervenes in good times and
  renders me defenseless
at the moment i am very upset about it but i cant do
  anything to stop it
it is like a poisonous snake roaming free looking out for
  me as a victim it is like a local anesthetic
i want to be rid of that anxiety
i want to be free of its clutches
i want to live and laugh and weep and see the things other
  people see

10.10.92

I don't want to be inside me anymore

rough ragged ideas kidstuff
and compulsive whirling idiot laughter
have to think about it first before i can think again
Question: HOW WAS IT AT THE CENTER TODAY?
i will tell you everything tomorrow
they will complain of poor birger and arrest him
he annoys everyone to the point of being defenseless and
    he is the worst of the autistics
i cant see any hope they all run off when they see me

                                                    10.12.92

what does a praiseworthy poet write on wednesday
when your inspiration has been fooled and is racing full
    tilt again
i cannot write poetry without resting in internal balance
otherwise i am a chattering madman

                                                    10.13.92

chosen birger will write
a long letter to chosen steely gisela tomorrow
but the long conversation was very impressive
i would very much like to talk too but i am a fool i rest in
    silent profundity*

                                                    10.18.92

*Arising from a telephone call with Gisela Ulmann.

a letter to totally important amazingly good gisela
dear dear gisela
at least someone knows what way we are thinking
when connections of time and space are so hard to explain
i cannot organize time like socalled normal people
i take my bearings from banal things like just mealtimes
    and times for going to bed and getting up
i cannot look for torn time
it is eternally extinguished from a realm engendering time
    and cannot be brought back
by torn time i mean the time at a persons disposal
and which pitilessly restlessly fills up my idiotic insanity
    in bucketsful within eternally unique uncertain
    uncertainties
i dont know any words in our language to describe this
    terrible phenomenon
is this important inexplicable crazy phenomenon the cause
    of my madness
thank you most fervently
your simple pupil birger

10.19.92

it is nonsense to say i couldnt stick it out long at the
    university
i mean i never had a chance to prove it
its true that studying psychology could give me mental
    stimulation
i think i will work along those lines first
i will do linguistics later

10.24.92

196

I don't want to be inside me anymore

for important reasons i want to write to gisela again
dear gisela
i read your letter all at once totally right
i am glad i put the question in a way which meant you
    understood what i was talking about
i do always want to answer factual questions correctly but
    i often dont feel calm while i am writing
i get agitated and nervous and keep wanting to run away
i can help myself out of this dilemma only by learning to
    tell factual questions and internal questions of the inner
    world apart
i always get worked up when i hear something very
    important full of ideas
and i will tell your plain honest self that i will find
    inaccessible ways of becoming a simple ordinary chosen
    person too
with all good wishes

10.26.92

i want to write a letter to leif*
i am so glad that you ask questions in your letter
i would humbly like to reply to you i can decipher any
    kind of writing
i am an incomparable fantastic knowall expert on
    handwriting
i dont want to exaggerate but i can read all usual kinds of
    writing
because the rewarding business of reading is vitally
    important for a mute person
i think you will understand that we are all looking for
    further general knowledge about our earth
one possible way was reading
i have read many extraordinarily impressive books since
    my fifth year of life
and i hoard all their important contents in me like
    precious treasures
i tell myself poems and stories
i interpret and that makes much of the contents of a poem
    visible
i make up many poems inside myself but not in a way that
    sticks to the laws of poetry
i have laws of my own they break the mold of careful
    smallminded plunderers of poetry
i call my art the inner art of all idiots and autistics
with our art we scale the peaks of the depths of the misery
    of human existence
let me conclude

*A schoolboy of seventeen who wrote to Birger.

I don't want to be inside me anymore

without language i am a poor madman and i can write
  only with the help of another person
  which is very humiliating and i am ashamed of it
dear leif i sent you my best wishes
kimusawea
that means dont adapt if your soul is dying inside you
from birger sellin

10.27.92

nonsensical knowall birger is pleased
to be known all over the world
lack of speech is not the same as lack of intelligence a
  speech inhibition can have various internal functions
  bringing peace inside you
i mean without certain knowledge of the theories known
  to no one theories from the depths of the autistic world
  you cant explain lack of speech or get a grip on it
it is a great problem because we need support while
  writing
i have no idea why that should be so

10.28.92

NOVEMBER

_____

it hurts so much inside to feel like an idiot again
at the university i behaved like an academic caveman[*]
i want to say something
i can imagine taking you into my world but on this
    condition
that i neednt fear being despised
i am so ashamed of all my silly mistakes
a film is bound to show them in a very unpleasant light[†]
i would rather show an internal world like an island
    guessing where the shores lie
entirely impersonal a fiasco a chaos
trembling this is very like a partly dead ruined city
i will be there as a destroyer and a bringer of nonsense
i work there like someone inventing panic to help
    restlessness
rise again successfully
one day i will tell you a story about that
i will certainly ruin everything outright
i will alarm judgmental citizens of earth with my dark
    stories

[*]Birger had a screaming attack while attending the Free University in Berlin.
[†]Jamila Chauvet was visiting and asking questions for the film.

I don't want to be inside me anymore

jamila will be afraid of me too
she has no idea of the crazy horrible reality in me
i am cruel and unfeeling
capable of anything bad
but unfortunately there is no good really wonderful
   extraordinary dropout
he has died and will not come back

11.2.92

everything is possible to a real autistic
because of effects arising from unknown reasons
we dont know any bounds
an autistic jumps hushabye baby out of his skin
and hushabye baby under his skin

11.4.92

i want to write a letter to uwe[*]
dear uwe
your letter made me very consciously acutely glad
i am really happy that another mute person can speak
i am sure we excellent crazy people will be taken back into
    glorious society
it is so important to be able to communicate in our
    valuable and excellent society which is by no means
    without its boxes
i am working on being accepted again
i am just working out my plans for a strategy i am sure we
    will need great dignity and courage to persuade other
    people that we can think in a human way and feel like
    other people
but with us a new generation of autistics will arise
we will come back from swamps of silence crying out
one very good idea i think is to write what happens to me
    in my world
good wishes and heartfelt understanding
from birger

11.13.92

[*]An autistic of Birger's age who writes by the facilitated communication
method.

202

I don't want to be inside me anymore

i must learn to weep
how can i bear the pain raging inside me without tears
i will write a song for injured people in the lonely
    luxuriant islands of sorrow
i will weep away your pain
be born again
find peace
water runs down my face
tears of pain
tears in the middle of the desert
an island of sorrow
always this corroding godless scream
one of a kind
from weeping driedup insatiable throats inner islands of
    sorrow
wounds festering on and on breaking out of a thousand
    inner springs
brooks of water will stream from a thousand inner springs
    and spread inner understanding island wisdoms
a healing water pours over the wounds

11.14.92

real extension of internal achievement i mean greater
    knowledge
brings more restlessness and compulsions with it
i cannot shift the knowledge
it ripens in me with difficulty and decays in me and stinks
i receive crazy orders sour as vinegar from the heart of the
    strange internal festering command center responsible

11.16.92

i will abandon all expressly extraordinarily remarkable
   seeking for ways
i will stay autistic and live like a crazy person in a society
   that scorns us modest souls
i will not make any more great efforts just to fail
i want to achieve everything within a short time
in my imagination i can do it all
but really it comes to nothing
i never want to do any more than simply write
just go to school
university is too much of a strain for me
i will try again later
my fear of screaming is too great
i want to be totally submerged in wild life sevenfold
i want to grace our theater in the city with my presence
   and sit through concerts
i want more art and literature

11.17.92

I don't want to be inside me anymore

i am eager to get rid of that eternal senseless idiotic
   thinking
i mean thinking along repetitive lines and with unending
   repetition of words
there is no point in the endless questions and answers
it makes me crazy myself
it is a silent occupation in my loneliness
what troubles me is that it has increased again
i can find no way out of this circle
one solution is intellectual discussion in the family
like over the last few days
that did me good
i have to think about it afterwards and that makes me
   calm
but i can hardly help myself
i am always getting into that pattern of unthought
i am a stereotypical fool

11.18.92

i want to write another letter to valuable gisela
dear incomparable gisela
i am very sad that i cannot come to your seminar
i may be able to come some other semester
i understood everything in our experiment very well
it was really exciting
all those new ideas about humanity about psychological
    ways of thought
i was very surprised and i want to know more about it
with very good wishes from
birger the untrained monkey man

11.19.92

your clever eager honest fear for your son birger isnt
   necessary
i am constantly working on fantastic systems for not being
   withoutme and staying inside me in my own world i
   am a homeless nogood top class traitor without
   character and in the world above i am an irresponsible
   new beginner and crazy
i expect long years of apprenticeship and journeying
no one can get to know an island person quickly
it is a long and very difficult way and you have to search as
   if you were in a labyrinth above all you need is patience
with this in mind i want to learn to be more careful of my
   own feelings and those of others and also to put a name
   to obvious mistakes and not just scream on my own
   account i am learning how to speak up when necessary
Question: DO YOU WANT THE TYPING ERRORS IN
   YOUR BOOK CORRECTED?
i would like all the insider typing errors removed but the
   beginning should stay as it is so that people can see how
   difficult it was to speak in real sentences

11.20.92

i am going to write a long letter to frau w.
dear frau w.
you live like almost no one else out of conviction
i feel upset by people who get by without convictions even
    in my immediate surroundings
there are people without personal opinions
however i dont want to talk about just any people at the
    moment but to say what i think about your opinion
i am not sure of the origin of my useless troublesome
    autistic sickness
i often think the cause is in the psychic or mental area and
    not any organic damage
it often seems to me as if i had too much energy in me
repeating crazy actions without control
and then i can do nothing about it
repetitions and compulsive behavior are giving me a lot of
    trouble again right now
i can find no rest
even the teachers in my institution assume i am a chaotic
    character but i am not that way on purpose
without control over what i do
producing nonsense out of a crate
birger sellin that unusual terrorist autistic sends you good
    wishes
he puts everything else in the shade
it is nonsense to think i am crazy and dont understand
i am crazy and i do understand which is even worse
it is nonsense that i am a good poet
i only rhyme cheese with peas and that doesnt taste good
im sorry but at the moment i cant stand myself and i call
    myself names it is very unconstructive and retards my
    development   *11.22.92*

I don't want to be inside me anymore

i want to write another useful letter to gisela
dear gisela
i was pleased that you visited us yesterday
i know you dont like visiting
you were very nice in a clearly untroublesome way
you accepted me but you didnt bother me
with social conventions like greetings
and other set forms of behavior which i cant master
i am very sorry that i wont see you at the university now
but at the moment my restlessness is too great my whole
    inside is in uproar
i can scarcely keep still for a few minutes
such physical meetings are a help to me
then i can make up a thousand songs for guests inside me
how much your face expresses
how intolerably wise your solutions for conditions in the
    crazy inner world are
i think about what you said
without your teaching nothing will come of me
i send good wishes
no one can be more grateful your amazingly shameless
    crazy birger sends good wishes
in all due form out of spontaneous heartfelt feelings
and in obvious agitation

11.23.92

i would be sorry if you crashed[*]
i would fall into another silence
and spend the rest of my life in an asylum
i like my present life even if it is very limited and you are
    lovable too and not so bad at all
whatever i may have said

11.24.92

it is really nice at home again
i would like to be independent and at the same time stay
    at home
it is really impressive at advent time
i am looking forward to tomorrow
a fabulous event coming soon is your terrific gingerbread
    house

11.28.92

[*]Birger's parents were flying to Hamburg for two days.

I don't want to be inside me anymore

i have been thrown out of the institution again
because they all say i didnt know what i wanted
because yet again nothing new would go right
Question: WHAT WOULD YOU LIKE FOR
   CHRISTMAS?
i would like a good edition of crazy nietzsche

11.29.92

DECEMBER

i cannot bear these relapses all the time
how come nothing helps me it is nonsense that its all to be
   in vain
i feel new confidence in myself
and a great belief that i will do it
i see progress too
for one thing i can say
something is too much of a strain for me
a simple phrase is so important to me
because i am overstraining myself
i suffer most from internal restlessness right now
it is bubbling and boiling inside me like in a witches
   cauldron underground
these are not internal noises from extraordinary physical
   activity
but a general psychic confused restlessness
coming on with crazy strong troublesome power
making me really go mad
times which are without anxiety isolate me much less
i keep repeating a sentence inside me for purposes of
   suggestion
let the anxiety go

I don't want to be inside me anymore

dont fight it
but the anxiety sticks symbiotically close
and wont just let me go
it is destroying me

12.1.92

dont you go crazy with all that washing every day
how do you manage to sort out such quantities so quickly

12.2.92

a skyblue fabulous primeval wish of all autistics is to give
    up their isolation and loneliness
and be recognized as a social species
we want to be autistic in such a way that
you normal people will feel it is interestingly exotic
and it wont get on your nerves

12.4.92

why is everything devoid of great joy again
i am sure jonas suffers because i am so changeable
and unfortunately dependent on addiction
i am sorry
i would like to be better about the house
and i will try to behave more calmly
but how glad my brother will be when he has a sensible
    randy brother fit for your nonsensical wishes i would
    like to get away from my crazy stinking autism for his
    sake too
i am making a personal declaration of intent here
its all over with the autism
i declare my retreat

12.5.92

i am an idiot how come i cant stand situations any more
    the way i used to its really bad
i want our film to show this contradiction
and the gulfs between the outside and inside world
partly its because the way is so very long
no one can say how important your cheerful help is its very
    valuable
but i want to rest inside me
i am wrong if poor straightforward birger thinks
he can free himself from autism
i am wrong about lonely people trying to switch to
    normality

12.9.92

I don't want to be inside me anymore

i liked it a lot in the city
time and people who arent hurrying impress me
i think one day i will know what its like just going around
    as a human being without any fictional autistic
    invention
any trembling waking
i realize i will live it cant be otherwise
i feel it
and i think hard about my situation
even if our outside world still doesnt notice anything
    without ways of seeing of the internal kind
it will do away with that
one day even wrongthinking people will get the idea

12.10.92

how does it look when i scream
people seem very upset and confused
how come the reactions are so bad
i dont by any means feel all the bad things i see on their
     agitated faces
i feel cast out by some bitter mistake
for in their faces i see
they would like to scream themselves scream for rage and
     fear and bafflement
the difference is
they darent hurt normal people
and bring confusion to the sad ordinary everyday world
but i am not hurting anyone when i scream
and i need to do it so much to get my balance
perhaps one day i wont always need it but now i am sure it
     is still important

12.11.92

I don't want to be inside me anymore

i will ruin myself first and then you
partly on purpose partly for no good reason
i feel bad and i would like to be good
but the evil always gets the upper hand
i am destroying our lives for no reason
again its just a question of venturing on a new beginning
i will have another shot at evaluating what happened
    today
i will make my way back groping from the world where i
    am beside myself
i am always discovering ways i have looked for islands
    whose shores i guess at
i would be lying
if i were to describe loneliness
as if it were something i wanted
loneliness is my enemy
and i will fight the good fight against it

12.13.92

probably everyone who sees my film
without inside knowledge
will say he is crazy
but our film should show internal realities
the reality of that very different autistic world
the recurrent endless troublesome thoughts images sounds
    and voices
nonsense streaming on and on in unending chainlike
    succession for years through the inner mind
we wander around lost in this chaos
with no sense of space and time
our areas of knowledge are islands
and so are tiny ways of escape like now like talking about
    the writing
i want to end this nonsense
and live a sensible life
i would love to be free of the groundless fears
i wish for nothing more fervently
i would accept anything for instance poverty and horrible
    surroundings
this is for janet and jamila
a real letter will follow but
i send you both good wishes in great and exquisite
    friendship
straightforward crazy birger restored to life
from berlin the great city on the edge of madness

12.14.92

for important reasons
i am writing to an eager lady frau w.
from your long letters i realize

I don't want to be inside me anymore

that you can think a lot of withoutme ideas
i like going into separate thoughts
i was particularly touched
that you think someone like me
can get to be a useful member of our society too
and i thank you for giving me courage
unfortunately i cant write any more
because i am too restless
i dont know why
the restlessness always overcomes me in situations
when i am not expecting it
i can be totally free of it only by writing
i live under such strain
that i often explode
which always means animal screaming
i cant manage without shouting
it limits my life so much
that i can only sit around somewhere
i destroy our family life at home
we cant talk together any more
and my screaming hangs in the rooms like a sword of
    damocles
i am so glad
that my incredibly thoughtful family members can still
    stand me
they even hope like me that i can be saved from the
    deepest depths
i thank all the people who keep hope alive in me the hope
    that i can be freed from my autism
and you in particular for your kind letters
your ever stupid incredibly confused crazy
birger sellin   *12.16.92*

219

island people degenerate
they see only their chosen world but isolated they will go
    mad from their hopeless steely
journey to the interior

12.20.92

i want to write to christoph*
from your poem i can feel
you are a withoutme poet
i like your poem very much
it comes from the depths of our autistic world
it has the true colors of our world
i will write you a poem about the joy of
being able to express yourself
i love language
it makes the inner world flower
it sends thoughts bold as an eagle into dimensions of your
    most secret inner dreams
it links those of us trapped in our loneliness
i am glad of your poem
it is like an ethereal transfer of lost thoughts within our
    worldly being that is controlled by
reason and under torture
i thank you in heartfelt earthly friendship and affection
good wishes from birger without himself but with you

12.21.92

*A twelve-year-old autistic boy who is writing by the facilitated communication method.

I don't want to be inside me anymore

i will write a christmas poem because i am happy
christmas has come again
a festival of safe harmony
a festival with the joyous aura
of its consecration confused joys
its sweetness cannot be measured
its festive dishes cannot be measured
strange sounds in the night
i love you you chaotic festival
our blessedly miming ordained feast of joy
i love you you incomparably beautiful dream festival
of love and happiness
i love the scent of the tree
the lights
and childish laughter
i love my childish family
who do all they can to stage a feast of illusion
endless love
crazy expense for a christmas dream
without craziness the tradition will die
the craziness will bear seeds of trouble within me
and will live on
people are so close to me at christmas
incomparable nonsense in sensible heads
i love you all particularly at christmas
when you are at least as crazy as me

12.22.92

i do firmly want to feel harmony again i ought to say that
    i am particularly afraid there wont
be enough presents
which is anxiety of a poor quality
seeing that ive never had too few presents yet

                                   12.22.92

christmas came again
a festival of harmony
a fantastic feast of play in incomparable ritualized patterns
    of illusion
i send my loving thanks to you
i enjoyed it very much

                                   12.24.92

there is one thing thats crazy
being in yourself is a dead state
being without yourself is loneliness
neither being in yourself nor without yourself can survive
there are no pure states
there is always change taking place in me
and even in calm times two forces that wont be reconciled
    are working

                                   12.25.92

I don't want to be inside me anymore

i want to reply to chosen uwe
dear uwe
your letter gave me great pleasure
i see you as a friendly correspondent
it is really good to hear from a mute person how you feel
    about the world
and i share your hope that one day we can talk to each
    other like everyone else
however i have noticed that we have the ability to speak
but it must be blocked somewhere
and this is why it is impossible for us to behave properly
    or write alone
it is less the organic area than the psychic area that is
    disturbed
i feel more and more sure of that
a relaxed psychic situation means i can do much more than
    when i am tense and anxiety is also the reason why
    writing wont work for some people
i am sure we will find a way to independence
i greet you cassandralike
that means in sympathetic respect
birger sellin
who is personally very close to you just as you are to me
    from afar

12.27.92

POSTSCRIPT

———

dear readers
thank you for getting right to the end
for persevering with my works
you would be wrong to think i am a great personality
i am only a withoutme figure who has stepped out of the
    darkness
of the autistic world to make contact with human citizens
    of your kind in the world
but i cannot take part in your life because my world still
    holds me prisoner
i am still looking for the way out to you
i long to do important things and i am racking my brains
    to think how someone can be freed as it were from
    prison
writing is my first step out of that other world
and i am glad that now a book has been made of it
i wish you a simple but internally whole and very loving
    life
your dark nonperson birger

Bibliography

Bettelheim, Bruno. *The Empty Fortress.* New York: Free Press, 1967.

Crossley, Rosemary, and Anne McDonald. *Annie's Coming Out.* Ringwood, Victoria: Penguin Books Australia, 1980.

Delacato, Carl H. *The Ultimate Stranger: The Autistic Child,* rev. ed. Novato, Calif.: Arena Press, 1984.

Park, Clara C. *The Siege.* Boston: Little, Brown, 1967.

Prekop, Jirina. *Hättest du mich festgehalten. . . .* Munich: Kösel-Verlag, 1989.

Sacks, Oliver. *The Man Who Mistook His Wife for a Hat and Other Clinical Tales.* New York: Harper & Row, 1987.

Stehli, Annabel. *The Sound of a Miracle.* New York: Doubleday, 1991.

Tinbergen, Niko and Elisabeth A. *Autistic Children: New Hope for a Cure.* London: Allen & Unwin, 1983.

Williams, Donna. *Nobody Nowhere.* New York: Doubleday, 1991.

Zöllner, Dietmar. *Wenn ich mit euch reden könnte. . . .* Munich: Scherz Verlag, 1989.